"Fiedler and his associates have provided more empirical evidence than any other training group which satisfies the requirements for evaluating training effectiveness.

"Leader Match is cost effective. Most leadership training programs require weeks, months, or even years without providing empirical evidence from controlled field experimentation that they actually improve the leader's performance on the job. Leader Match, however, requires no more than 4 to 12 hours of training time. It represents an inexpensive and promising new development in an area that up to now has been frustrating and unsatisfactory."

K.H. Wexley and Gary P. Latham, *Developing and Training Human Resources in Human Organizations*.

IMPROVING LEADERSHIP EFFECTIVENESS:

THE LEADER MATCH CONCEPT
SECOND EDITION

Fred E. Fiedler
Martin M. Chemers

A Wiley Press Book
John Wiley & Sons, Inc.
New York · Chichester · Brisbane · Toronto · Singapore

Library of Congress Cataloging in Publication Data

Fiedler, Fred Edward.
  Improving leadership effectiveness, 2nd.

  (A Wiley self-teaching guide)
  Bibliography: p. 257
  Includes index.
    1. Leadership—Programmed instruction.   2. Supervision
of employees—Programmed instruction.   I. Chemers,
Martin M.   II. Title.   III. Series:
Self-teaching guide.
HM141.F46   1983   303.3'4'077   83–6741
ISBN 0–471–89213–0

Printed in the United States of America

84 85 10 9 8 7 6 5 4 3 2 1

This book is dedicated to

Judith Fiedler and *Barbara Chemers*

CONTENTS

ACKNOWLEDGMENTS

Improving Leadership Effectiveness has now been in use since 1976. It has been successfully tested in a wide variety of civilian and governmental organizations in the United States and abroad, and we have learned a great deal in the intervening years about its strengths and weaknesses. We have also found new ways for presenting the material in the course of giving workshops and training programs. It seemed time, therefore, to rewrite this manual in light of this extensive experience.

Since its original publication, a new generation of students, colleagues, and coworkers has contributed greatly to our understanding of the principles and concepts on which this program is based, and we have profited from the many comments of those who have taken Leader Match training. We are especially indebted to Roya Ayman, Patrick J. Bettin, Dean Frost, Joseph E. Garcia, and our erstwhile collaborator and co-author, Linda Mahar, for their invaluable contributions to this revision. Special thanks are due Sarah M. Jobs who not only contributed to the substance of the program but also took considerable responsibility for preparing the manuscript for publication. Dewey L. Blyth, Deanna Dicomes, Judith Fiedler, and Joseph E. Garcia gave us constructive criticism of the final manuscript.

Many organizations we worked with in training programs graciously permitted us to collect data and provided extensive feedback on the effectiveness of the program. We should like to express our particular thanks to Fire Chief Robert Swarthout and Chief Pletan as well as many others of the Seattle Fire Department: to Deputy Chief Ben Andrus and Assistant Chief Ken Curtis of the Salt Lake City Fire Department; to Paul Watson, Ed Wall, and Anne Currier of the National Fire Academy; to Cam Albin, Herb Price, Ted Sheil, and Jack Blair of the Texasgulf Corporation; and Frank Smith and Robert Rhode of Sears Roebuck. Finally, our thanks to the officers and noncommissioned personnel of both the 9th Army Division and ROTC Region IV. Their cooperation enabled us to test Leader Match under highly controlled conditions.

We are indebted to Margaret Sokol and Marci Brown for their assistance in preparing the manuscript for publication, and to our editor, Judy V. Wilson of John Wiley and Sons, for her support and assistance. Finally, we wish to acknowledge with much regret that other commitments made it impossible for the coauthor of the first edition, Linda Mahar, to contribute again to the present edition. Her ideas are still very much a part of this book.

FOREWORD

One of the most difficult personnel decisions in management is what sort of person to promote into a leadership position. The familiar cliche that what individuals have done in the past is the best indication of what they will do in the future is almost useless because there are no data on previously demonstrated managerial capabilities. True, there may be information on community projects and similar off-the-job situations, but translation is difficult and at times irrelevant. As a result, selections are frequently made on the basis of excellence in former, different assignments. The best engineer may thus become a supervisor or the best toolmaker a foreman. While technical capability is certainly desirable and even critical, we have learned to our sorrow that it is not enough for successful leadership which places a premium on interpersonal skills.

The 1940s and 1950s saw a serious attempt to use personality tests to identify the human qualities most likely to be associated with managerial success. Personality inventories, self-ratings, and interest checklists were widely administered. The early ones were generally straightforward, simple to take and score. As it became apparent that intelligent people could adjust their results to project their perception of the desired personality, more and more complex instruments were developed to obscure the meaning of responses. Gestalt techniques such as the Rorschach inkblot test and the Thematic Apperception Test were tried. For these instruments the skill and judgment of the interpreter were critical and their cost discouraged wide usage. The more fundamental problem, however, was that all these devices assumed that personality characteristics could be measured and that some were "good" and others "poor" for leadership purposes. For the most part, correlation of success with the results of such tests proved to be so low that their value was questionable. Moreover, present Equal Opportunity regulations severely limit their use.

The next wave of research was focused on defining successful managerial style. Much was learned about the impact of style on subordinate performance. Most researchers seemed, however, to be seeking a single "right" or "appropriate" style (although psychologists probably would not admit it).

Undoubtedly influenced heavily by McGregor's Theory Y of management, many managers in the Fifties and Sixties engaged in workshops, self-analysis, and group exercises in an attempt to analyze their style and modify it to become more "democratic." Some success can be claimed for this effort, although much reported improvement in interpersonal sensitivity was on the home front, rather than at work. In business or industry, lack of reinforcement from superiors or associates was often given as the reason for failure to implement good resolutions. In any event, the impact can best be described as mixed.

Throughout this period Fred Fiedler conducted his research. He looked not only at individuals and how they behaved, but also at the kind of situation in which they were functioning well or badly. Because of this dual focus on person and situation, the desirability of more than one leadership style to accommodate a variety of situations became clear. To those of us working in the selection field it provided a blinding flash of insight. His research matched our experience! All of us had seen at least one highly successful individual fail when moved to another position which required the same or similar technical strength. And, of course, all of us had observed a wide variety of successful styles among members of management. What Fred Fiedler's work did was to make it possible for people to focus on understanding and accepting their own style and recognizing its positive and negative effects, rather than trying to change their style. As a personal strategy this surely offered considerable promise.

There was just one problem. With all the good intentions in the world, it was very difficult to get a reliable reading on one's style or, if one were obtained, to know how to evaluate situational factors.

This Self-Teaching Guide, *Improving Leadership Effectiveness*, helps resolve the dilemma. Fiedler and his associates not only supply a quick understanding of the philosophy and underlying theory of leadership (with appropriate disclaimers of miracles), but also provide a straightforward, nonthreatening way for a person to rate himself or herself on a number of style factors. They then supply a series of rating scales for evaluating situational characteristics so that appropriate matches can be made between the two. The concept has already made a distinctive contribution to management *thinking*. The devices proposed for rating and comparative purposes may also make a unique contribution to management *action*.

This book is of interest and help to individual workers who are considering a leadership position. It is equally useful to personnel placement and organizational development specialists concerned with recommending qualified candidates for open positions. It is valuable to persons already in a supervisory or managerial position who should feel continuing concern about leadership capability, both their own and that of their subordinates. Of special interest to executives is Part IV "Management of Managers." Here are suggested ways of analyzing the styles of subordinate managers to determine the kinds of working situations that are likely to help them achieve success. It sheds light on that difficult top management concern: "How can I influence the results achieved by managers in my organization without interfering with their own methods and practices?"

If I seem enthusiastic about this book, it is because I believe it fills a great need and will be useful to a large number of present and aspiring leaders and their mentors.

Marion S. Kellogg
Vice President,
General Electric Company

PART I

IDENTIFYING YOUR LEADERSHIP STYLE

1

INTRODUCTION TO LEADER MATCH

The quality of leadership, more than any other single factor, determines the success or failure of an organization. This is true of a small work group, a large organization, or even an entire nation. Without the inspiring leadership of George Washington, the Revolutionary War might have been lost. Without Winston Churchill's dogged determination, Great Britain as we know it might well not have survived. Without Abraham Lincoln, the United States may well not have held together.

Leadership is no less important in business and industry. Men like Henry Ford or Andrew Carnegie determined the fate of their enterprises. The remarkable recovery of the Chrysler Corporation is credited largely to Lee Iacocca. And the newspapers speak almost daily of corporate battles in which one person makes decisions that affect thousands of employees and stockholders.

But effective leadership is equally important in less grandiose enterprises. To the family that has sunk its life's savings into a restaurant, store, or service station, the effectiveness of the manager frequently means the difference between financial security and disaster. And the leadership of a volunteer organization or service club determines to an even greater extent whether it will accomplish its goals or see its membership melt away.

Leadership has been the topic of intense speculation and controversy for thousands of years. Indeed, Plato's *Republic* is a treatise on national leadership. The fact that we are still conducting research on leadership tells us that we are dealing with a very complex problem. If there were simple answers, we would have known them a long time ago.

We have learned a great deal about leadership in the last few decades, however, and we are beginning to understand what makes leaders successful. This short manual is designed to teach you how to become a more effective leader or manager.

What Do We Mean by Leadership?

Basically, the leadership role or function involves the motivation, direction, supervision, guidance, and evaluation of others for the purpose of accomplishing a task. This task may be something the group wishes to do or, more typically, it is assigned by the organization of which the group is a part. The leader is usually expected to make decisions for members of his or her group that determine the group's actions. The effectiveness of a leader is usually measured on the basis of ratings given by immediate supervisors or, whenever possible, by measuring the performance of the leader's group.

This book is designed to improve your effectiveness as a leader. You must recognize, however, that leadership also may involve counseling of subordinates, managing conflict, inspiring loyalty, and setting ethical standards. This book does not deal explicitly with these related issues, but other good sources of information on these topics are available and should be consulted if you feel the need. In this book we concentrate on the effective performance of the task for which the group or organization was assembled.

What Will This Program Do for You?

This self-instructional manual will help you to become a more effective leader. It is based on the well-established fact that an individual may be an extremely effective leader in one situation and fail in another. General George Patton was one of the most outstanding tank division commanders in World War II, and Florence Nightingale was one of the outstanding administrators of nursing organizations. It seems doubtful, however, that Miss Nightingale would have made a good tank division commander, or General Patton a good leader of a hospital ward.

There are any number of business executives who were highly successful in one organization, but who failed in another. Some executives perform exceptionally well in getting an organization started, but cannot successfully manage its routine operation afterwards.

The important point is that you cannot expect to excel in all leadership situations. In this regard you might want to remember one important thought: *If you learn to avoid situations in which you are likely to fail, you are bound to be a success.* This book will teach you to do so.

What Is New About the Leader Match Approach?

This leadership training program is based on the "Contingency Model of Leadership Effectiveness," a theory developed over the last thirty years. This theory states that a leader's success is contingent on two factors: (1) the leader's typical way of interacting with members of the group (i.e., the leadership style); and (2) the degree to which the leader has control over the situation (i.e., the group, the task, and the outcome). We call this "situational control."

It is very difficult to change personality or long-established behaviors. We know only too well how little success has been reported in trying to remake husbands, wives, or children, and how difficult it is to break a habit like smoking. The way we interact with our subordinates and superiors is learned from childhood on, and is no more easily changed. However, we do know that people behave differently in different situations, and that it is frequently very easy to change critical aspects of our leadership situation. This program teaches you how to manage your leadership environment, your situational control, rather than how to change your personality or interpersonal relations with subordinates.

Why is situational control important? When you feel in complete control of your leadership situation you are relaxed, secure, and at ease. You may even be bored. When you are not in complete control of everything, when the outcome of your actions is in doubt, there is an element of tension, uncertainty, and perhaps excitement. When your control is very low, that is when you are anxious about what might happen next, when you have no idea what needs to be done about it, you then feel tense and anxious.

The reason why a change in the leadership situation is likely to affect your performance then becomes easy to see. A moment's reflection will tell you that most people act quite differently when they are relaxed and secure than when they are tense, insecure, and anxious.

The above is a very important point. Lack of situational control affects your behavior and ability to function. Some people perform best when they are relaxed and at ease, when everything is under control. But there are others who need challenge and excitement, who need to have their juices stirred up. They want risk and uncertainty—they go to race tracks and on mountain climbing expeditions; they work best under deadlines and want a life that presents problems. This book will show you how to identify your leadership style and "engineer" your leadership situations so that they match your personality by providing the amount of situational control that is just right for you.

What Is the Basis for This Leadership Training Program?

The contingency model, which is based on studies going back to 1951, was first published in 1964. Since that time more than 400 journal articles and book chapters have been written about it, and the contingency model has become one of the most researched and best validated leadership theories. A detailed analysis of all studies testing the contingency model shows overwhelming support for the theory (e.g., Strube and Garcia, 1981).

The theory tells us that effective leadership depends on the leadership situation as well as the individual. When we say that leaders are made, not born, we mean that nearly everyone can be effective in some situations. We have collected data on well over 3000 leaders, and there are very few, indeed, who have not been effective at some time in their life. This book is, first and foremost, a practical guide to effective leadership, and we will talk about theory and principles only insofar as these are required to understand the training program.

Throughout this manual, we shall also assume that leaders must be technically qualified to perform their job. No matter how well trained a person might be in leadership techniques, no one should perform a triple heart bypass without surgical training, or command an airliner without a commercial pilot's license.

What Does This Program Require of You?

You will benefit from this manual only if you read carefully and work through the various exercises and quizzes. A training program cannot make you more effective unless you understand it. We expect that it will take you only six to ten hours to complete this book, depending on how much you know already, and how fast you want to get through. However, programmed instruction definitely cannot be read like a novel!

CAUTION—DO NOT SKIM THE MATERIAL. DO NOT SKIP SECTIONS YOU MUST UNDERSTAND EACH SECTION BEFORE YOU MOVE ON TO THE NEXT SECTION

Not even the best cookbooks and highly structured work guides will give you answers to all possible problems. You will have to know underlying principles so that you can apply them in situations not covered by this short manual. Be sure you understand the material.

How Is This Program Organized?

This book contains four major parts:

1. Part I shows you how to identify your particular style of leadership, and the behaviors that go with it.

2. Part II teaches you how to diagnose leadership situations.
3. Part III tells you how to change critical elements of your leadership situation so that they will match the particular requirements of your leadership style.
4. Part IV shows you how to apply the contingency model to work situations involving your own subordinate managers—how to help them to perform better. It also discusses a variety of related issues that will assist you on becoming a more effective leader.

The end of this book provides a list of additional reading, and a selected list of published studies dealing with the contingency model and Leader Match training.

How To Get Started?

Each chapter begins with a brief discussion of a particular principle or its applications. This discussion will be followed by exercises, called "probes," which help you to understand the new material.

Each probe presents a leadership problem to illustrate the main points of the chapter. It is followed by several alternative solutions. Choose the best answer, and then turn to the following page for feedback. The feedback page tells whether or not you made the correct choice and discusses the answer. If your response was correct you will be directed to go on to the next probe or to the next chapter. If you did not choose the best answer, the feedback page will advise you to reread certain parts of the book. You should then try to answer the probe again.

You may find it useful to read through the feedback for all the right and wrong answers to each probe since they discuss why certain responses are right and others miss the mark. We suggest you keep a bookmark handy while you check your answers and review appropriate material. Do not become disappointed or discouraged if you do not immediately get the best answer on each probe. This is a learning process, not a speed reading exercise, and some mistakes are not only inevitable but necessary if you are to learn efficiently.

Each chapter ends with a short summary that will help you review the material when you return to the book after taking a break. For this reason, you may find some of the summaries repetitious. However, some repetition is helpful for remembering the most important points in the material.

Each part includes a self-test to let you know whether you are ready to go on to the next chapter. A final test will help you to evaluate your overall understanding of the program.

We recommend that you space your study over at least two or three days. The best breaking points are the ends of each part.

AGAIN, DO NOT SKIP OVER CHAPTERS!

It is essential that you take each chapter in sequence, and that you understand a chapter before moving on to the next.

ONWARD!

A Technical Note for Interested Readers

The following discussion deals with the evaluation of Leader Match training, its effectiveness for women and members of minority groups, and its usefulness for training in other cultures. The section also discusses the major reasons for the present revision. If this is not of interest to you, you may safely skip to Chapter 2.

Why Are We Revising This Training Program?   A large number of Leader Match training sessions and workshops have been conducted since Leader Match was first published in 1976. These have enabled us to improve the material as well as our approach. We have also identified some important conditions in which leaders are able to make effective use of their abilities and experience, and we have incorporated this material in Chapter 12. Finally, a number of other investigators have conducted research to test the effectiveness of Leader Match training. Thus far, all of these studies have shown that Leader Match increases managerial performance and the effectiveness of organizations. Since we do not expect you to buy a pig in a poke, we will briefly describe some of these studies.

How Effective Is Leader Match Training?   One of our highest priorities has been a scientifically sound evaluation of Leader Match to determine its effectiveness. Although there are innumerable leadership training manuals and books on how to be an effective leader, very few have been adequately tested. In fact, Latham and Wexley (1981) called it the only leadership training program that has been adequately tested.

Evaluations asking trainees how they liked the training, how interesting it was, and how much they thought they learned are undoubtedly helpful since a program has to be acceptable to those taking it. But these testimonials by themselves provide very little basis for believing that the training will actually improve performance. Not a few Americans of 100 or 150 years ago swore by the effectiveness of swamp oil. The buyer of a leadership training program is entitled to more than testimonials that trainees liked it.

Leader Match has now been successfully tested in at least nineteen different studies conducted in various settings, with widely different groups of leaders and managers, and with various degrees of experimental control. Thirteen studies have already been described in major scientific journals (see Fiedler and Mahar, 1979a; Fiedler, Chemers, Bell, and Patrick, 1984; Frost, 1983).

All of these studies compared leaders who had been randomly selected either for training or for a control group. In each of these studies, trained and untrained leaders were subsequently rated by their supervisors or peers. The former was perceived as being more effective than the latter for as long as one year after the training was concluded.

One recent study of a soda ash mine in which Leader Match training was used found that the number of accidents and injuries showed a dramatic decline of about 50 percent. At the end of a three-year period productivity was 13.2 percent higher in tons per man hour than the average of other soda ash mines in the country (Fiedler, Bell, Chemers, and Patrick, 1984).

Four other studies are briefly described here to illustrate the effectiveness of Leader Match training. These sections are followed by a discussion of the appropriateness of Leader Match for women and members of minority groups in leadership and management positions, and for other countries. Subsequent sections deal with the development of norms for various scales you will be using in this manual. Again, if this does not interest you, go on to Chapter 2.

Second-Level Managers of a Public Health Volunteer Organization. Two successive studies compared second-level leaders of a large organization (Los Amigos de las Americas of Houston), which at that time sent 200 to 400 young people to Central and South American countries each summer to establish and conduct innoculation and immunization clinics. The volunteers worked in small teams, and three to five teams were supervised by older, more experienced men and women. One group of teams worked during the first three weeks of the summer while the second group worked during the next three weeks. Thus there were two sets of performance evaluations for second-level leaders.

These second-level leaders were divided at random into two groups: one received Leader Match training; the second received a programmed management training manual of about the same length. At the end of the summer, the second-level leaders were evaluated by their superiors on various aspects of their performance. In both studies, the trained leaders were rated as being significantly better in managerial skills. In both studies, the teams supervised by leaders with Leader Match training were rated as having performed better than teams supervised by leaders who were in the control group (Fiedler and Mahar, 1979a). Figure 1–1 shows the results of the second study comparing leaders with Leader Match to those with alternative training. The figure shows that the ratings of Leader Match trained leaders were above average while those of alternatively trained leaders fell below the average of all teams.

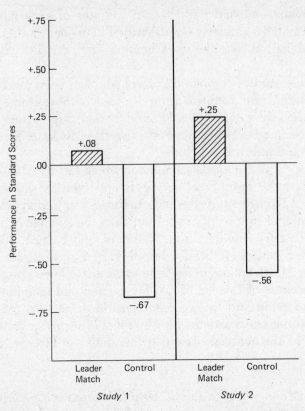

Figure 1–1   Performance ratings of public health organization leadres with Leader Match and with alternative training.

Executive Trainees at Sears-Roebuck.   The Sears company maintains five stores in the Midwest that prepare college graduates for careers in Sears retail department stores. The training lasts nine months, and the successful graduates are then employed by various other stores throughout the chain as division managers. Sears randomly chose two of the five stores for eight hours of Leader Match training. The same amount of time was devoted to management training discussions in the other stores. All stores, including the three in which Leader Match was not given, provided the usual training, including lectures and on-the-job training.

Seven months after the conclusion of training, all former executive trainees (now division managers) were rated by their new store managers and staffs on eight performance scales developed by the company. Those who had received Leader Match were rated as superior on each of the eight separate scales (Mahar, Rhode, and Fiedler, unpublished.)

West Point Cadets.   The US Military Academy, as part of its training program, sends cadets in their third summer to various army battalions where they serve as acting platoon leaders. At the end of the summer, the cadets are rated on their performance by their battalion commanders.

A group of fifteen cadets was randomly divided into thirds. One third of the men were given the Leader Match manual to read before being sent off on the field assignment; one third were given no information, and one third were told only that they would be controls in a training experiment. Despite the very small additional investment in time (i.e., 6–8 hours), those who had received Leader Match training performed substantially better than those who had not (Csoka and Bons, 1978). Figure 1–2 shows the average performance ratings received by cadets who had read through the Leader Match manual and those who had not been given the manual (Figure 1–2).

This study is of particular interest since we are dealing here with young men who had been completely immersed in intensive leadership training on a daily basis for several years. Nevertheless, a few hours of reading the manual substantially improved their performance in the field.

Male and Female ROTC Cadets (Fiedler and Mahar, 1979a) In order to determine, among other things, the comparative effectiveness of Leader Match training for women, we conducted a large training experiment with Reserve Officer Training Corps (ROTC) cadets. We randomly selected eighteen of the forty-six colleges and universities in the region that provided ROTC training and in which at least four female cadets would be enrolled in thirty-day advanced training camp during the summer. We then randomly selected nine of the eighteen schools in which all cadets received Leader Match training, and used the other nine schools as a control group. At summer training camp, cadets from all forty-six schools were randomly assigned to training platoons of fifty with no more than two cadets from the same school in the same platoon.

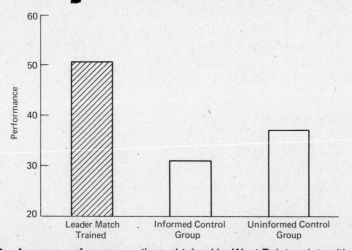

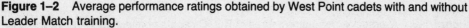

Figure 1–2 Average performance ratings obtained by West Point cadets with and without Leader Match training.

The advanced camp provides third-year cadets with field training under seasoned army officers who also evaluate the cadets for commissions in the regular army. The cadets also rated each other on their leadership performance. The training is strenuous, and the cadets are highly motivated to do well in their various tests. These tests include exercises on four or five separate days during the month in which a particular cadet might serve as squad leader, platoon leader, or company commander.

The results showed that male and female cadets who had received Leader Match training commanded significantly higher performance ratings than those who had been assigned to the control group. Leader Match training was as beneficial for female cadets as it was for their male counterparts. Figure 1–3 shows the average performance ratings obtained by cadets in the nine schools randomly selected for Leader Match training and for the nine schools in the control group. The graph shows that seven of nine schools in the former group received average scores above the mean of the eighteen schools in the study, while eight of the nine schools in the latter group received average scores below the mean.

Cadets who had understood the training, as shown by a comprehension test given prior to coming to camp, performed better than those who obtained lower scores on the comprehension test. In other words, those who had understood the principles of the training performed better than those who did not understand the training program. In addition, cadets who reported that they used Leader Match training obtained higher performance ratings than those who made little use of the training. These results are shown in Figure 1–4.

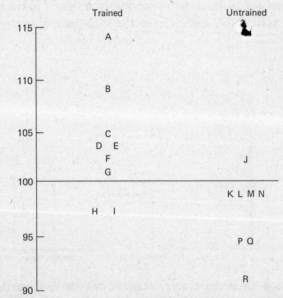

Figure 1–3 Average performance scores of ROTC cadets from schools with and without Leader Match training.

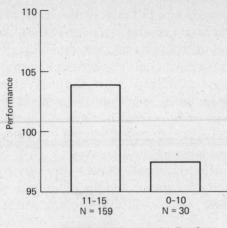

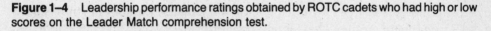

Figure 1–4   Leadership performance ratings obtained by ROTC cadets who had high or low scores on the Leader Match comprehension test.

Use of the Training Program by Various Organizations   The program has been used by a large number of military, civilian, and governmental organizations in the United States and in other countries. These have included academies of military and paramilitary services in the United States and abroad, the U.S. Civil Service Commission, and now the Office of Personnel Management, local and state governments, mines, department stores, social and health services, volunteer medical groups, and many more.

Norms for Scores Used in This Manual   We have accumulated normative data from a variety of groups. These data will assist you in better understanding your own leadership style scores and the way in which your own leadership situation differs from that of others. For example, we would expect a military officer to have higher position power than a professional supervising other professionals. We also would expect task structure to be higher in a production plant than in a research laboratory. To give you some reference points, we have listed the average scores for some representative groups.

Many readers and trainees have asked whether people in different occupational groups (e.g., the police, government executives, hospital personnel, etc.) tend to have different leadership styles as measured by our Least Preferred Coworker or "LPC" scores. We have not found these differences to be great or reliable, but we are again listing the average scores of various groups in Chapter 2 to show the range of these mean scores within each group. Note, however, that there are very great variations in scores within each group.

Women in Management Positions   One of the most striking developments in the management area in recent years has been the large influx of women and minorities into positions of leadership. Most women managers are still in lower and middle levels of management, but more will soon be represented in top management jobs as they attain greater seniority in their organizations.

The future increase in women managers can be anticipated from the steadily rising number of women in business and engineering school programs from which most managers are drawn. Thus, the proportion of women students in business has gone up in some business schools from about 4 to 6 percent in the 1960s to about 40 percent in 1982. While the total number of women in engineering schools was a mere handful in 1960, the proportion in some engineering schools is now over 30 percent.

To give just one further example, women currently represent about 8 percent of the U.S. military personnel, and the proportion is expected to rise to 12 percent. Many of these women will obviously attain high rank as they gain in seniority.

For the above reasons we have been particularly concerned with the appropriateness of Leader Match for women. A large number of studies have been conducted on the behavior and the performance of women in leadership positions (see Bass, 1981). These studies found some differences in the way women behave, and some studies, but not all, have found differences in the way women perform. It is difficult to assess the extent to which these differences reflect biases of the men as well as those of the women who rate women in leadership positions, or whether some real differences exist. Our own research provides no basis for believing that women are less effective than men as leaders or managers.

The highly controlled study on Reserve Officer Candidates, described above, indicates that Leader Match is as effective for women as for men. Other studies, as well as various training programs in which women participated along with men, provide every reason to believe that Leader Match improves the leadership and managerial performance of women as well as that of men.

Managers from Minority Groups   Data for members of minority groups also have been obtained in the course of various studies, and managers from various minority groups have participated in almost all of the training programs and controlled studies we conducted. Again, we found no evidence or reason to believe that members of minority groups exposed to Leader Match training benefitted less than did other trainees.

Leader Match Training in Other Countries   Leader Match has been translated into Japanese, German, and Swedish, and the English language edition has been used in such countries as Holland, Belgium, Mexico, and Canada, as well as various training institutes abroad. We have been told by users that the program is considered to be effective, and that its use is spreading.

Furthermore, the contingency model, the theory on which Leader Match is based, has been tested extensively abroad. There have been no major differences in the results obtained in the United States and in various other countries, including Germany, the Netherlands, Belgium, Japan, Thailand, India, and Czechoslovakia. It is, therefore, reasonable to believe that Leader Match will be as effective in these other countries as it is in the United States.

2

YOUR LEADERSHIP STYLE

Chapter 1 told you that your performance as a leader depends primarily on the proper match between your leadership style and on the control you have over your work situation. This chapter will help you to identify your leadership style and the conditions in which you will be most effective. Carefully read the following instructions and complete the Least Preferred Coworker (LPC) Scale on page 19.

INSTRUCTIONS

Throughout your life you have worked in many groups with a wide variety of different people—on your job, in social clubs, in church organizations, in volunteer groups, on athletic teams, and in many others. You probably found working with most of your coworkers quite easy, but working with others may have been very difficult or all but impossible.

Now, think of *all the people* with whom you have ever worked. Next, think of the *one person in your life* with whom you could work least well. This individual may or may not be the person you also disliked most. It must be the one person with whom you had the most difficulty getting a job done, the one single individual with whom you would least want to work—a boss, a subordinate, or a peer. This person is called your "Least Preferred Coworker" (LPC).

On the scale below, describe this person by placing an "X" in the appropriate space. The scale consists of pairs of words that are opposite in meaning, such as *Very Neat* and *Very Untidy*. Between each pair of words are eight spaces that form the following scale:

Very Neat _____ Very Untidy

    8   7   6   5   4   3   2   1

Think of those eight spaces as steps ranging from one extreme to the other. Thus, if you ordinarily think that this least preferred coworker is quite neat, you would write an "X" in the space marked 7, like this:

Very		X						Very
Neat	8	7	6	5	4	3	2	1	Untidy
	Very Neat	Quite Neat	Some- what Neat	Slightly Neat	Slightly Untidy	Some- what Untidy	Quite Untidy	Very Untidy	

However, if you ordinarily think of this person as being only slightly neat, you would put your "X" in space 5. If you think of this person as being very untidy (not neat), you would put your "X" in space 1.

Sometimes the scale will run in the other direction, as shown below:

Frustrating _____ Helpful

    1   2   3   4   5   6   7   8

Before you mark your "X", look at the words at both ends of the line. There are no right or wrong answers. Work rapidly; your first answer is likely to be the best. Do not omit any items, and mark each item only once. Think of a real person in your experience, not an imaginary character. Remember, it is not necessarily the person whom you liked least, but the person with whom it is (or was) most difficult to work. Ignore the scoring column on the right margin of the page for now.

Now go to the next page and describe the person with whom you can work least well. Then go on to page 20.

LEAST PREFERRED COWORKER (LPC) SCALE

Left	8	7	6	5	4	3	2	1	Right	Score
Pleasant	8	7	6	5	4	3	2 (X)	1	Unpleasant	2
Friendly	8	7	6	5	4	3	2 (X)	1	Unfriendly	2

Left	1	2	3	4	5	6	7	8	Right	Score
Rejecting	1	2 (X)	3	4	5	6	7	8	Accepting	2
Tense	1	2	3 (X)	4	5	6	7	8	Relaxed	3
Distant	1	2 (X)	3	4	5	6	7	8	Close	2
Cold	1	2 (X)	3	4	5	6	7	8	Warm	2

Left	8	7	6	5	4	3	2	1	Right	Score
Supportive	8	7	6	5	4	3	2 (X)	1	Hostile	2

Left	1	2	3	4	5	6	7	8	Right	Score
Boring	1	2 (X)	3	4	5	6	7	8	Interesting	2
Quarrelsome	1	2 (X)	3	4	5	6	7	8	Harmonious	2
Gloomy	1	2 (X)	3	4	5	6	7	8	Cheerful	2

Left	8	7	6	5	4	3	2	1	Right	Score
Open	8	7	6	5	4	3	2 (X)	1	Guarded	2

Left	1	2	3	4	5	6	7	8	Right	Score
Backbiting	1 (X)	2	3	4	5	6	7	8	Loyal	8
Untrustworthy	1	2	3	4	5	6 (X)	7	8	Trustworthy	6

Left	8	7	6	5	4	3	2	1	Right	Score
Considerate	8	7	6	5	4	3	2 (X)	1	Inconsiderate	2

Left	1	2	3	4	5	6	7	8	Right	Score
Nasty	1	2 (X)	3	4	5	6	7	8	Nice	2

Left	8	7	6	5	4	3	2	1	Right	Score
Agreeable	8	7	6	5	4	3	2 (X)	1	Disagreeable	2
Insincere	8	7 (X)	6	5	4	3	2	1	Sincere	2

Left	1	2	3	4	5	6	7	8	Right	Score
Kind	1	2	3	4	5	6 (X)	7	8	Unkind	3

| | 8 | 7 | 6 | 5 | 4 | 3 | 2 | 1 | | |

Sum 48

19

DID YOU ANSWER ALL THE QUESTIONS ON THE PRECEDING PAGE?

If not, do so before you read further.

WHAT IS YOUR LEADERSHIP STYLE?

To determine your LPC score, go back to the page with the LPC scale. As you will note, there is a number under each scale point. Note the number under the scale point on which you marked your "X". For each line, write that number in the scoring column at the right margin of the page. Then add your scores and enter the total at the bottom of the page. Be sure to check your addition!

Although you described another person, the score on the LPC scale tells more about you than about the person you described. We are not very accurate in our perceptions of others. (Just think of the many times you have heard remarks about you with which you completely disagreed!)

Your score on the LPC scale does tell a lot about yourself. It is a measure of your leadership style. It tells something about your basic goals and priorities in a work setting—that is, what you feel you must accomplish to be satisfied with yourself and your performance. Let us first use your score to identify your own leadership style, and then examine other leadership styles more closely.

- If your score is 73 or above, you are a high LPC person. We call high LPC people RELATIONSHIP-MOTIVATED
- If your score is 64 or below, you are a low LPC person. We call low LPC people TASK-MOTIVATED
- If your score fell between 65 and 72, you are a middle LPC person whom we call SOCIO-INDEPENDENT

The person who has a low LPC score describes the least preferred coworker in very negative, rejecting terms such as unfriendly, uncooperative, or cold. In effect, the low LPC person tells us,

"Work is extremely important to me; therefore, I have no patience with a poor coworker who prevents me from getting the job done. I find it hard, if not impossible, to accept or put up with anyone who is incompetent or unwilling to pitch in. It is so important that it washes out any other good traits or characteristics the coworker might have. If you frustrate me from getting the job done, you are just generally no good."

This is a strong emotional reaction to people with whom a low LPC person cannot work. For this reason, those with low LPC scores are called task-motivated.

The high LPC leader says something quite different:

"It is true that I can't work with you. But that doesn't mean that you might not be a friendly, sincere, or pleasant person. We may disagree at work but that doesn't mean we wouldn't enjoy a game of golf or racquet ball after work."

In other words, the task is important, but not so important that the high LPC person rejects the least preferred coworker as an individual. The high LPC person says,

"I may not be able to work with you, but you may be a good guy in other respects. I would not mind being with you, as long as we don't have to work together."

This type of person is more interested in good relationships with other people. That is why we call the high LPC leader relationship-motivated.

The people with scores between about 65 and 72 are more difficult to describe clearly. In fact, there are several reasons for obtaining a middle LPC score. Some people who fall just over the borderline may, in fact, belong to the task- or relationship-motivated group. Other people in this middle group may have a mix of motivations and goals and, therefore, they are harder to classify. Still others are of a quite different breed. They are less concerned with the opinions and judgment of their peers, and more likely to go their own way.

Your middle-LPC score will not indicate to which of these groups you belong. If your score falls between 65 and 72, you will need to determine for yourself which LPC type fits you best. You will be able to do this from reading the descriptions on the following pages.

You should be aware, of course, that descriptions of this type always exaggerate the good and the poor, the desirable and undesirable characteristics that distinguish people. It is sometimes easier to recognize your own and other people's leadership type by using less flattering descriptions than by just noting good points. Therefore, do not be put off because your leadership type doesn't make you out to be a paragon of virtue. None of the descriptions does, as you will see. These are caricatures and stereotypes rather than descriptions of real people, which thus emphasize distinguishing characteristics.

Whatever your score, note carefully that the high, middle, and low LPC leaders are very effective in the particular situations that match their leadership style. No single type is outstanding in all situations. We cannot stress this point too often. All leadership types have good and bad points, and each will be effective in the right situation. And all types of leaders are, on the average, about equally liked or disliked by their subordinates, again depending on the situation.

Let us now consider the typical behavior of people who score high and low on the LPC scale. For obvious reasons, these people are easier to tag than those who fall into the middle group. You will, of course, want to see how well these descriptions seem to fit you. However, don't expect to find every characteristic of the high or low LPC person in yourself or in others whose LPC score you happen to know. As we said before, these sketches are stereotypes. Their only purpose is to give you a feeling for how the typical high or low LPC person tends to behave in various situations.

One further point: Some people find it hard at first to recognize themselves in the descriptions, or they may identify more closely with the other leadership style. For example, you may have thought of yourself as more concerned with the task than with people, or alternatively, more with people than with the task. This is normal. Remember, we often do not see ourselves as others do. Think of a time you heard yourself on a tape recorder or saw yourself on videotape or in a home movie. It was probably startling, or even shocking, to meet yourself in this manner. Also, you undoubtedly have known some bosses who thought of themselves as kindly, open-minded, patient, forbearing . . . but who could not have recognized themselves by the comments of their subordinates.

Above all, our behavior depends in large part on the type of situation we find ourselves in. If you consider yourself to have the opposite leadership style, you may be thinking of your behavior in a relaxed situation, not a tense one. More will be said of this below.

Whatever your first impression might be, the LPC score tends to be fairly accurate in reflecting a leader's personality in various situations. Remember that nobody is perfect. The secret of effective leadership is to recognize your strengths and to make the most of them. The following descriptions fit various types of leaders:

RELATIONSHIP-MOTIVATED LEADERS
(LPC Score of 73 and above)

High LPC leaders derive major satisfaction from good personal relations with others. In fact, they need good relations in order to feel at ease with themselves. Their self-esteem depends in large part on how other people regard them and relate to them. As a result, high LPC people are concerned about what others think, and they are sensitive to what their group members feel. In a work setting, relationship-motivated leaders encourage group members to participate in decision making and to offer new ideas or a different approach to a problem. They usually do not get upset when things are complicated and they may like situations that require creative problem solving.

As you well know, our behavior is not static. We do not always behave the same way in all situations. For example, some people become withdrawn and shy when they feel insecure while others become bossy and noisy. Some people handle stressful situations by remaining calm and self-controlled while others tend to fall apart. Some people respond to stress on the job by throwing themselves into their work while others get rattled, withdraw, or seek encouragement and support from their coworkers.

It is important to recognize how a person behaves when everything is under control, but it is even more important to understand and predict how this same person will behave in an uncertain, uncontrolled situation. The key to understanding leadership effectiveness is in understanding and recognizing predictable changes in behavior that occur in response to the environment. Armed with this knowledge, we can engineer leadership situations to maximize our performance and minimize our mistakes. Later we will discuss in detail how to tell whether a situation is high, moderate, or low in control, and what situational control means to you, the leader.

For the moment, you should note that situational control indicates the degree to which a leader feels certain of being able to get the job done. This feeling of certainty depends in large part on the leader's relationship with the group, on the structure of the task, and on the power vested in the leader's position. Shortly, we will speak of high, moderate, and low situational control. However, a detailed discussion of the concept will not be presented until Part II of this book.

Let us first consider how the RELATIONSHIP-MOTIVATED, high LPC person reacts under conditions of high, moderate, and low situational control.

• *In low control situations* (situations that are stressful for some people and challenging for others), high LPC leaders look for support from their group members. They will be considerate of subordinates' feelings, nonpunitive, and concerned with the welfare of the group. The high LPC leaders thus may pay less attention to the task. They can become so concerned with seeking the support of the group that they fail to get the job done. In extremely stressful situations, high LPC leaders may withdraw from the leadership role altogether and not give the direction that the group needs.

• *In moderate control situations*, relationship-motivated leaders are really in their element. The situation has just enough uncertainty to challenge them, yet not enough to make them lose sight of the job. The high LPCs' concern with their group members' feelings enables them to get the group's support in performing the task. If group conflict exists, or if the group's support of the leader is lukewarm, the relationship-motivated person is able to work around it by being tactful and sensitive to problems before they become damaging to task performance.

• *In high control situations*, the leader does not have to worry about the group's support and about how to do the job. Under these conditions, relationship-motivated leaders are likely to feel bored and unchallenged. Some high LPC leaders react to this situation by becoming involved with details and reorganizing the work. They also may try to control group members too much. They tend to become stricter, more concerned with discipline, and heavy-handed in their management, and thus are often seen by subordinates as bossy. Some high LPC leaders may seek to impress their superiors by issuing a lot of orders and by giving very detailed instructions, even when such actions are not needed. As a result, their performance tends to suffer.

TASK-MOTIVATED LEADERS
(LPC Score of 64 and below)

Task-motivated (low LPC) people find their main satisfaction in getting things done. They gain more self-esteem from concrete achievement than from their relations with others. They feel most comfortable when they can work from clear guidelines and standard operating procedures. If these guidelines are missing, the low LPC leader will try to create them.

• *In low control situations*, task-motivated leaders concentrate on the job. They don't worry too much about what others think of them, and are able to work well even if they have little support from their group members. Under these conditions, their main concern is to control their group. As a result, when things get tough, low LPC leaders may seem harsh and punishing in their need to complete the task.

Low LPC leaders are no-nonsense people who are likely to take charge early and start organizing things. In committee meetings, they tend to move right in and get down to business—sometimes before group members have had time to explore all the issues and to consider all the alternatives. Generally speaking, low LPC leaders are quick to assign tasks, make up schedules, and check on progress. Group members may not always like low LPC leaders' way of going about the job, but the group generally respects them for getting results under difficult conditions.

• *In high control situations*, when they know that the job will get done, task-motivated leaders relax and let themselves take time to socialize and consider the feelings of their group members. They are pleasant and friendly. Task-motivated people find satisfaction when things are going well and enjoy the feeling that everything is running just as it should. In high control situations, they take the opportunity to learn more about their group and about how to do the job even better.

• *In moderate control situations*, which often involve personal conflict, task-motivated leaders tend to be less effective. They find these situations stressful and difficult to handle. They may bury themselves in their work rather than dealing with the needs of their group members. They find it more difficult than high LPC leaders to handle personal conflicts and personality clashes, and their subordinates sometimes interpret this as a lack of concern.

SOCIO-INDEPENDENT LEADERS
(LPC Score 65–72)

The middle-LPC group, as we said earlier, is much more difficult to describe than either the high or low LPC groups. Generally speaking, middle-LPC leaders appear to be somewhat detached, and more inner-directed, less distracted or concerned by what others may think, but more open to their environment. They are, therefore, more flexible and learn more from their experience, and they make better use of their abilities under many conditions.

The performance of middle-LPC leaders is generally good, in situations in which they enjoy high control. They perform less well when situational control is low. As time goes on, we will, undoubtedly, learn more about the behavior of this particular group.

ARE THERE OCCUPATIONAL DIFFERENCES IN LPC?

One of the questions that occurs quite naturally is whether certain types of occupations call for different types of leaders. For instance, do effective military leaders tend to have different LPC scores than business executives, hospital personnel, or those who went into government service? And are certain leadership styles more typical of one culture than another?

The answer to both of these questions, as far as we can determine, is no. It is, of course, always difficult to say whether a scale in a foreign language is identical to an English language scale. We, as well as some of our colleagues, have conducted research in Greece, Thailand, Iran, Holland, and Belgium. Additional studies have been done in other countries as well. The LPC scores obtained in most countries seem to be quite comparable to those in the U.S. Scores obtained in Iran were higher than those obtained in the U.S.

As to the first question, whether different occupational groups tend to have different LPC scores, the answer is again, no. Listed on p. 26 are average LPC scores obtained for a number of different occupational groups. There are, of course, some differences from group to group. These appear to be chance fluctuations since no statistically significant differences were found between LPC scores for the groups listed below. In general, then, these averages give no indication of systematic major differences between occupational groups.

To summarize, the Least Preferred Coworker scale measures an individual's primary goal or motivation in a work setting. All leaders have concern

TABLE 2–1 Average Scores Obtained for Various Occupational Samples

Population Sample	Average LPC
Second level Managers, Iran	84.03
Head Nurses, U.S. and Canadian	80.80
Fire Fighters Urban Fire Department	71.50
Second Level Managers, Mexico	71.40
Hotel Managers,	71.25
Lieutenants, Urban Fire Department	69.57
Captains, Urban Fire Department	68.67
Public School Principals	66.37
National Guard Senior Officers	64.09
State Executives, reporting to the Governor	64.00
Battalion Chiefs Urban Fire Department	63.12
Battalion Staff Officers U.S. Army	62.30
Company Commanders, U.S. Army	60.32
State Executive Assistants	57.96
Administrators, City Treasury Office	52.00

for both tasks and relationships. However, in any one situation, different types of leaders will emphasize these concerns differently. For example, in a low control situation, the task-motivated leader's main concern is to get the job done while the relationship-motivated leader will first seek the support of the group. In a high control situation, the task-motivated leader will have time to be involved with the group because he or she knows the job is getting done while the relationship-motivated leader will show more concern for the task. The "true" middle-LPC leaders are a separate type. Rather than being high LPCs whose scores happen to be below the cutting point, or low LPCs with higher-than-normal scores, they tend to be more independent of the opinions and judgments of others. They are less involved in interpersonal relations and hence are more open to their environment.

On the average, low LPC people are as well liked as are high LPC leaders. They do not necessarily have poor personal relations with their group members. After all, many people like bosses who run a "tight ship" and don't get personally involved with them.

The descriptions of relationship-and task-motivated leaders are useful in understanding the different approaches to leadership. However, whether you are a "true type" or a combination of leadership styles, remember that your effectiveness as a leader will depend on how well your style fits your leadership situation, not on whether you score high or low on the LPC scale.

The following tables provide a handy reference guide to TYPICAL behavior of task- and relationship-motivated leaders across low, moderate, and high situational control.

TABLE 2–2 Behavior of Relationship-Motivated Leaders Under Low, Moderate, and High Situational Control

Low	Situational Control Zones Moderate	High
*Nonpunitive	*Considerate of Group Members	*Punitive
*Seeks Group Support	*Participative in Decision Making	*Creates or Changes Work Assignments
*May Withdraw from Job Altogether	*Rallies Group To Task Accomplishment	*Directive and Controlling

TABLE 2–3 Behavior of Task-Motivated Leaders Under Low, Moderate, and High Situational Control

Low	Situational Control Zones Moderate	High
*Punitive	*Directive and Controlling	*Nonpunitive
*Directive and Controlling	*Insensitive to Group Member's Needs	*Relaxed and Supportive of Group
*Organizes Work Assignments	*May Withdraw From Group—Concentrates on Task	*Participative in Decision Making and Problem Solving

Now try the following probes to see how well you have understood the discussion of leadership styles. Choose the best answer and then turn to the following page for feedback.

PROBE 1

You have just read about the leadership styles measured by the Least Preferred Coworker scale. Which of the following statements best describes the LPC score?

    ____ a.   It is a measure predicting that a person will behave in one particular way in every leadership situation.

    ____ b.   It measures behavior that changes constantly from situation to situation with little consistency or predictability.

    ____ c.   It indicates the needs and goals that a leader will see as most important in various leadership situations.

Go to the next page for feedback.

FEEDBACK

a. **You chose (a):**   *It is a measure predicting that a person will behave in one way in every leadership situation.*

> This is not correct. While the LPC score predicts an individual's motivation, it does not show that an individual will behave the same way in every leadership situation. Remember that relationship-motivated (high LPC) leaders are very considerate of subordinates when they are not in control of the situation; when they are in complete control, they may be inconsiderate and bossy. Likewise, task-motivated (low LPC) leaders are relaxed and easygoing when they are in complete control. In low control situations, they become concerned with the task and neglect personal relationships.

Put a bookmark at Probe 1 to hold your place. Then reread Chapter 2 and try Probe 1 again.

b. **You chose (b):**   *It measures behavior that changes constantly from situation to situation with little consistency or predictability.*

> This is incorrect. If the leader's behavior was so unpredictable and changeable, there would be little purpose in measuring it. We could not use LPC as a measure of personality affecting group performance in various situations.

Put a bookmark at Probe 1 and then reread Chapter 2 and try Probe 1 again.

c. **You chose (c):**   *It indicates the needs and goals that a leader will see as most important in various leadership situations.*

> This choice is correct. We cannot predict a single individual's behavior with complete accuracy. However, the LPC score gives us a general idea of a leader's goals and motivation. Different types of leaders have different goals. They also perceive and react to leadership situations differently. The LPC measure is an important step in matching leaders and situations for maximum effectiveness.

Now try Probe 2 on the next page. You're doing fine!

PROBE 2

The foreman who works for you has just taken the LPC scale and tells you that this measure can't be any good. He has a high LPC score and is, therefore, supposed to be concerned with interpersonal relations. However, he doesn't get along with everybody and he is certainly concerned with the task because he works hard. *What would you say?*

_____ a.   The foreman does not understand the nature of the LPC score. He assumes that a high LPC person will always behave in the same way, and therefore, that LPC can't be any good.

_____ b.   The foreman's score is probably in error since he works hard and is concerned with the task. This suggests that he is more likely to be low LPC.

_____ c.   The foreman probably misunderstood the scoring system. A person with a high LPC score is concerned with the task and not with relationships.

Go to the next page for feedback.

FEEDBACK

a. **You chose (a):** *Your foreman does not understand the nature of the LPC score. He assumes that a high LPC person will always behave in the same way, and, therefore, that LPC can't be any good.*

This is most likely the right answer. The foreman did not correctly understand the nature of the LPC score. It measures the importance a person assigns to task and interpersonal goals, and not specific behaviors. As you may remember, in some situations high LPC people do not get along with their subordinates because they become too absorbed in trying to please their boss. In relaxed, well-controlled situations, high LPC leaders sometimes work hard and concentrate on the task. At other times, in situations of moderate control, they are more concerned with interpersonal relationships.

The foreman mistakenly assumed that high LPC leaders always behave in the same way. In addition, of course, it is very difficult to see one's own behavior clearly. Most people are surprised when they learn how others describe them. Therefore, although he may have felt he did not typify a high LPC leader, his goals or motivational system (and his behavior as seen by others) was typical of the high LPC individual.

Turn to page 35 and complete Probe 3.

b. **You chose (b):** *Your foreman's score is probably in error since he works hard and is concerned with the task. This suggests that he is more likely to be low LPC.*

This answer is not correct. High LPC leaders also are concerned with the task, otherwise they would not be successful in any situation. Moreover, neither high LPC people nor anyone else can necessarily "get along with everybody." In fact, in situations in which they have a high degree of control, high LPC people are sometimes seen as bossy and arrogant. In these situations they also pay a good deal of attention to the task, although they are not necessarily most effective. The points made by the foreman would certainly not be sufficient to think that his LPC score was in error or that it is not a good measure.

Reread the descriptions of the two styles of leaders on pages 20–27 and then try Probe 2 again. (Use a bookmark to hold your place at Probe 2.)

c. **You chose** (c):   *The foreman probably misunderstood the scoring system.
A person with a high LPC score is more concerned with the task and not with
interpersonal relationships.*

> This is incorrect. A high LPC score *does* indicate concern with interpersonal relationships while a low LPC leader is more concerned with task accomplishment. Therefore, the foreman did not misunderstand the scoring of the LPC scale.

You missed on this one, try Probe 2 again after rereading the descriptions on the two styles of leaders on pages 20–27. (Use a bookmark to hold your place at Probe 2.)

PROBE 3

Your supervisor is generally a very relaxed person, especially as long as he has everything under control. However, since he got a new boss, you have noticed a change in him. You now find that he has really tightened up on discipline. He immediately wants to take formal action against anyone who does not shape up. He also has become very directive and goes around issuing orders. He is likely to be:

_____ a.   Relationship-motivated.
_____ b.   Task-motivated.

Go on to the next page for feedback

FEEDBACK

a. **You answered (a):**   *Relationship-motivated*.

 This is not correct. The relationship-motivated leader under the stress of having to adjust to a new boss would tend to seek the support of his coworkers and subordinates and he would be less concerned with the task.

Better review Chapter Two and try Probe 3 again.

b. **You answered (b):**   *Task-motivated*.

 This is quite correct. The supervisor is likely to be task-motivated. You probably recognized this from several parts of the description. First, the supervisor was quite relaxed when he felt in control. Low LPC leaders are indeed relaxed when they know that the job will be accomplished. They can then take it easy and let things take their course. Secondly, a new boss poses a threat. The supervisor does not know what demands the new boss will make; he does not know how he will get along with the new boss; and what kinds of assignments or standards he will have to live with. Finally, your supervisor became very directive. This is his way of dealing with the problem of a new boss—tightening up his control and discipline.
 High LPC leaders would react quite differently. When they are faced with having to relate to a new boss they need the emotional support of their group members and they will, therefore, let up on discipline to avoid antagonizing the group members.

You're doing well; continue on to the next probe on the following page.

PROBE 4

Larry Berger has been office manager for two years. He has been known as a guy who didn't let his people get away with too much: he kept an eye on things, and he did not hesitate to reprimand people when they deserved it. He also tended to be somewhat aloof from his subordinates and spent a lot of time with his boss.

He recently was transferred to a new office where he has a similar job but somewhat more responsibility and less control over his situation. Interestingly enough, he now seems to be unwilling to maintain any discipline, he doesn't want to give any reprimands or take any other action. He also has become much more friendly with his subordinates. You would diagnose him as:

____ a. Relationship-motivated.
____ b. Task-motivated.

Go to the next page for feedback.

FEEDBACK

a. **You chose (a):**   *Relationship-motivated.*

> You are quite correct here. This is the typical pattern we find in relationship-motivated persons. When all goes well and they enjoy a great deal of control and influence, they can be task-masters and concerned with tight discipline as a means to impress their boss. They also tend under these conditions to neglect their relations with subordinates and become concerned with their boss and others. This causes them to appear aloof and distant to subordinates. However, a new job, and the need to establish positive interpersonal relations with a new boss and new subordinates creates uncertainty and lower situational control in relationship-motivated leaders. They then are very reluctant to alienate their group members, sometimes to the point of letting them get away with infractions which they would never have allowed before.

You seem to understand the two types of leadership style. Please go on to page 39.

b. **You chose (b):**   *Task-motivated.*

> This is not correct. Task-motivated leaders, as you will recall, become concerned with the task when they are in a low control, less certain situation. Consider the problems new supervisors have on a job: They must establish themselves with their new boss, supervise new subordinates, and learn something about the job. Under these conditions task-motivated leaders become quite concerned with their ability to accomplish the task, and they therefore tighten, not relax, discipline. They also tend to devote all their energies to their task, often to the detriment of their relationships with their employees.

Reread the sections on relationship- and task-motivated persons (pages 22–25) and try Probe 4 again.

SUMMARY

The best way to identify your leadership style is to complete the Least Preferred Coworker (LPC) scale. The LPC scale indicates which goals or motivations are important in a leadership situation. These different goals and motivations cause behavior to vary as the situation changes. Although all leaders are concerned with tasks and relationships, high and low LPC leaders emphasize them differently depending on the situation. The summary below reviews the two different leadership styles.

RELATIONSHIP-MOTIVATED—
High LPC (Score of 73 and above)

Generally, high LPC leaders are more concerned with personal relations, more sensitive to the feelings of others, and better at heading off conflict. They use their good relations with the group to get the job done. They are better able to deal with complex issues in making decisions.

• In high control situations, relationship-motivated persons tend to become bored and are no longer challenged. They may seek approval from their superiors, or they may try to reorganize their work. As a result, they often become inconsiderate towards their subordinates, more punishing, and more concerned with performance of the task.

• In moderate control situations, relationship-motivated leaders focus on group relations. They reduce the anxiety and tension of their group members, and thus reduce conflict. They are also patient, considerate, and concerned with the feelings and opinions of their group members. Thus, they handle creative decision-making groups very well. High LPC leaders see this situation as challenging and interesting and perform effectively in it.

• In low control situations, relationship-motivated leaders become absorbed in obtaining group support often at the expense of the task. Under extremely stressful situations, they may also withdraw from the leadership role, failing to direct the group's work.

TASK-MOTIVATED—
Low LPC Leaders (Score of 64 and below)

Generally, low LPC leaders are more concerned with the task, and less dependent on group support. They tend to be eager and impatient to get on with the work. They quickly organize the job and have a no-nonsense attitude about getting the work done.

• In moderate control situations, task-motivated leaders tend to be anxious and less effective. This situation is often characterized by group conflict, which low LPC leaders do not like to handle. Low LPC people become absorbed in the task and pay little attention to personal relations in the group. They tend to be insensitive to the feelings of their group members, and the group resents this lack of concern.

• In high control situations, task-motivated leaders tend to relax and to develop pleasant relations with subordinates. They are easy to get along with. As long as the work gets done, they do not interfere with the group or expect interference from their superiors.

• In low control situations, task-motivated leaders devote themselves to their challenging task. They organize and drive the group to task completion. They also tend to control the group tightly and maintain strict discipline. Group members often respect low LPC leaders for enabling them to reach the group's goals in difficult situations.

If your score falls into the borderline area between about 65 and 72, you must carefully analyze your leadership style as you learn more about the two types.

You have now learned to identify leadership motivations, and have determined your own leadership style. Remember that no single leadership style is effective in all situations. Rather, certain leadership styles are better suited for some situations than for others. The next part will show how to measure the amount of control various situations give the leader. You will also learn to identify the situations in which you are likely to lead most effectively.

Now try the Part I Self-Test on the next page.

PART I SELF-TEST

Indicate whether the statements below are true or false.

____ 1. The leadership styles measured by the LPC scale are behaviors that do not vary in different situations.

____ 2. Low LPC, task-motivated leaders are generally less well-liked by their followers than are other types of leaders.

____ 3. High LPC, relationship-motivated leaders are primarily motivated to gain esteem from other people.

____ 4. Low LPC leaders are most comfortable in situations where the task is clearly defined and orderly.

____ 5. High LPC leaders generally try to avoid conflict by carefully managing interpersonal relations.

____ 6. In low control situations, low LPC leaders are more critical and give more orders than high LPC leaders.

____ 7. Under predictable and relaxed conditions, low LPC leaders are likely to act nervous, edgy, and distracted.

____ 8. Low LPC leaders tend to be most productive in very high control situations or in very low control situations.

Go to the next page for the answers to this Self-Test.

Answers to Part I Self-Test

False 1. *The leadership styles measured by the LPC scale are not behaviors that remain the same even if the situation changes.* Although a leader's needs and motivations will remain relatively constant, different leaders will use varying strategies or behaviors for satisfying these needs as leadership situations change.

False 2. *Low LPC, task-motivated leaders are not generally less well-liked by their followers than are high LPC leaders.* Both types are about equally well-liked by their followers.

True 3. *High LPC, relationship-motivated leaders are primarily motivated to gain esteem from other people.* High LPC leaders gain self-esteem when other people (followers, peers, superiors) like them and judge them to be competent.

True 4. *Low LPC leaders are most comfortable in situations where the task is clearly defined and orderly.* Low LPC leaders do indeed function most effectively and feel most relaxed when the job demands are clear. A clearly defined job gives them a better chance to gain esteem from successful task achievement.

True 5. *High LPC leaders generally try to avoid group conflict by carefully managing interpersonal relations.* By and large, this statement is true. High LPC leaders are sensitive to the personal atmosphere in their group. They try to head off conflict and maintain pleasant work relations.

True 6. *In low control situations, low LPC leaders are more critical and give more orders than high LPC leaders.* When low LPC leaders are under pressure, they strive to create an orderly task environment. They do this by assigning jobs, directing work, and closely monitoring performance.

False 7. *Under predictable and relaxed conditions, low LPC leaders are not likely to act nervous, edgy, and distracted.* When situations are clear, predictable, and controllable, low LPC leaders feel relatively assured that they can satisfy their needs. They then become relaxed and considerate with followers.

True 8. *Low LPC leaders tend to be most productive in very high control situations or in very low control situations.* Low LPC leaders seem to perform best under very predictable conditions when task demands are very clear and under very uncertain conditions where their direction and no-nonsense style gives order to a chaotic situation.

PART II

IDENTIFYING LEADERSHIP SITUATIONS

3

YOUR LEADERSHIP
SITUATION

As we have said, the effectiveness of leaders and their groups depends on two major factors: 1) the underlying motivation of leaders; that is, the type of goals most important to them (leadership style); and 2) the degree to which they can control and influence their leadership situation.

There are certain leadership situations in which you will be much more effective in than others. There are some people who can manage highly routine operations that require constant attention to detail. There are others who need variety and challenge in their jobs. Some people perform best when they can set their own work pace; others need tight deadlines.

It is extremely important that you learn to recognize the particular conditions and situations in which you are most effective as a leader, and those conditions that are not your particular cup of tea. This chapter and those immediately following will tell you how to diagnose your leadership situation. A later chapter will also show you how to modify these situations so that they will fit your particular style and leadership approach, thereby maximizing your effectiveness.

What do we mean by "leadership situation?" The underlying basis for classifying a leadership situation is the degree to which it provides leaders with control and influence—the degree to which they can predict and determine what their group is going to do, and what the outcomes of their actions and decisions are going to be. It also means that the leader can predict with a high degree of certainty and assurance what will happen when he or she wants something done.

There are three primary components that determine control and influence in the situation:

1. *Leader-member relations:* The degree to which the group supports the leader.
2. *Task structure:* The degree to which the task clearly spells out goals, procedures, and specific guidelines.
3. *Position power:* The degree to which the position gives the leader authority to reward and punish subordinates.

These dimensions can be combined in various ways to describe the amount of situational control in any leadership position. For example, if a construction superintendent builds a bridge from a set of blueprints with the full support of subordinates, he or she knows that the job will almost certainly get done. The task itself may be difficult, but it is clearly spelled out by blueprints and specifications. Hence, the superintendent will have no doubts about the way in which he or she must go about the job and what the results should look like. In this situation, the construction superintendent has a great deal of control and influence.

In contrast, consider a task such as chairing a Parent-Teachers Association committee to "organize a picnic that everybody will enjoy." This task itself may seem easy, but the leader has very little control. The group members are likely to be volunteers who can, if they want, walk out on the committee at any time. The person in charge has no power to make them work, and it is always difficult to predict in advance whether everybody will in fact enjoy the picnic.

The three components, leader-member relations, task structure, and position power are used to measure the amount of control in a leadership situation. For purposes of the discussion, the leadership situation is then divided into three "zones" or types of situation: 1) high control; 2) moderate control; and 3) low control. An example of a high control situation, as mentioned above, would be that of the construction superintendent who builds bridges. He has a great deal of control and influence in this situation because a reasonable certainty exists that (a) subordinates will willingly follow instructions because he or she has their full support, (b) a set of blueprints and specifications will be available to tell him how to proceed at each step, and what the final product should be, and (c) he can discipline those who fail to do what they are told. This situation, as we shall see, would provide only moderate control if the superintendent's subordinates did not accept him.

Another example of a moderate control situation would be a research team developing new products. In this situation the leader may have the support of the team, but no one can predict the best procedure or whether the final product will be successful; that is, whether it will be adopted and ultimately be profitable. Also, research team leaders frequently find it difficult to fire or discipline scientists on whom they must depend for creative research. Therefore, their control is at best only moderate. If the leader is not accepted, control would be low.

Before you begin the actual measurement of these three important components—leader-member relations, task structure, and position power—read the brief descriptions of each on the following pages and then answer the probes.

LEADER-MEMBER RELATIONS

The *most important* single element in situational control is the amount of loyalty, dependability, and support you, as the leader, get from those with whom you work. If the group is sincerely trying to assist you in getting the job done, and is following the spirit as well as the letter of your directions and policies, your control will be quite high. If you have the group's support, you don't need to rely as heavily on your position power or task structure to get compliance; group members already accept your direction and are eager to do what needs to be done. Such a leadership situation is, therefore, likely to have either high or moderate control.

Conflict with the group demands a great deal of time and effort. If you are the leader of an antagonistic group, you must constantly be on guard to make sure that people will do their work right, and even that no one will try to sabotage your efforts. When you are unsure about your group's loyalty and dependability, you must be on your guard and rely more heavily on position power and the structure of the task in order to get the job accomplished.

Also important is the support you get from your boss. If your boss accepts and supports you, group members are more likely to hold you in esteem, and to accept your leadership. If your recommendations to your boss are accepted and approved, your group members will have more confidence in you as their leader. For some leaders this is one of the most important aspects of a leadership situation.

TASK STRUCTURE

The second most important dimension of control and influence concerns the structure of the task. How clearly is it spelled out, are the goals known, is there a clear and accepted procedure for performing the job? Some tasks or assignme. ts are spelled out in considerable detail and in a way that allows little or no deviation. Many people get very anxious and upset if they get a job and don't know exactly what is to be done and how their work will be evaluated by their boss or by others whose opinion matters. Most of us like to know what we are supposed to do and that we've got a good chance to finish a job that has been assigned. This is, of course, much easier if the task is highly structured than if it is vague and unstructured.

To go back to an earlier example, building a bridge would be a highly structured task. The construction superintendent will have a set of detailed instructions, specifications, and drawings that must be followed. At certain points along the way the work will be inspected and approved, and final engineering tests will determine whether the bridge is ready for use.

In contrast, a school picnic can be organized many different ways. No one can predict whether a particular plan will be successful or unsuccessful until it is implemented. And certainly, there are no infallible rules or methods for organizing a picnic. This is, therefore, an unstructured task, as is every task that requires creativity, resourcefulness, and important decision-making functions. Task structure is the most complex of the three dimensions making up situational control.

POSITION POWER

The third element in determining your situational control is the power the organization vests in your leadership position for the purpose of directing subordinates. You will usually find high position power in line jobs of most military, business, and industrial organizations. These jobs typically include foremen, line managers, and supervisors who direct relatively routine production-oriented tasks. It also includes most leaders with middle or lower level command responsibilities in military and paramilitary organizations.

As the chairperson of a committee or the leader of a group performing creative or nonroutine tasks, you will generally have lower position power since you need to depend on others to give you their willing cooperation. Relatively low position power is sometimes found in organizations such as university departments, advisory boards, or research teams in which the members have a strong voice in management. It also occurs in professional organizations in which the leader must depend on senior employees for advice and assistance. In these situations it is very difficult to pressure such key subordinates as your legal counsel or your chief economist or the only technician who can program your computer.

Again, the support you enjoy from your superiors is important. If you can get your recommendations accepted, get your people promoted or get them good assignments, your power in the eyes of your subordinates will be higher than if you have little or no influence with your own boss. If subordinates can readily go over your head to the next higher level, you will have very little power to manage your group.

Although position power usually comes to mind first when we think about situational control, research has shown that it is the least important of the three aspects we have discussed. For example, no matter how much power and authority you have, it is hardly ever enough to prevent sabotage by a disgruntled subordinate or to evoke more than grudging effort from an uncooperative group (those who doubt this should consider the problems of managing prison labor). For this reason, position power is given relatively less weight than either leader-member relations or task structure.

MEASURING SITUATIONAL CONTROL

The next four chapters will show you how much situational control your current leadership job gives you. These chapters will tell you in detail how to measure the three situational control dimensions—leader-member relations, task structure, and position power.

Now try the probes on the following pages.

PROBE 5

Based on what you have just read about situational control, which of the following statements is *most* accurate?

_____ a.   A leader's influence and control with subordinates is determined primarily by formal organizational authority—position power.

_____ b.   The structure of the group's task is the most important determinant of the leader's control and influence—task structure.

_____ c.   Leader control is a vague and complex phenomenon that cannot be measured.

_____ d.   A leader's control is dependent upon several factors in the situation, most importantly acceptance by group members—leader-member relations.

Go to the following page for feedback.

FEEDBACK

a. **You chose (a):**   *A leader's influence and control with subordinates is determined primarily by formal organizational authority—position power.*

This is incorrect. In fact, formal authority is usually less important than other situational factors. As you will recall, a leader's power and authority are rarely great enough to prevent the sabotage of a group by a disgruntled subordinate or to evoke more than the minimal amount of effort from an uncooperative group.

Review Chapter 3 and try Probe 5 again.

b. **You chose (b):**   *The structure of the group's task is the most important determinant of the leader's control and influence—task structure.*

This answer is not correct. It is true that a leader's control will be increased to the extent that he or she understands the demands of the task and can assign members to specific duties. However, this is not the most important determinant of the situation.

You had better reread Chapter 3 and try Probe 5 again.

c. **You chose (c):**   *Leader control is a vague and complex phenomenom which cannot be measured.*

As you will see in the next four chapters, this is incorrect. If it were true that the leader's control is so complex that measurement is impossible, this training program would also be impossible. While leadership situations are often complex and, therefore, difficult to classify, we have been able to measure the degree to which they give the leader control and influence.

You've missed the point. Read Chapter 3 again, then make another choice of the alternatives given in Probe 5.

d. **You chose (d):**   *A leader's control is dependent upon several factors in the situation, most importantly acceptance by group members—leader-member relations.*

Correct! The influence and control of leaders is increased to the degree that they can count on all group members to do their job as well as possible (leader-member relations). This is the most important dimension in determining situational control. The clarity and specificity of job demands (task structure) and the leader's power to recognize and reward good work (position power) combine with leader-member relations to determine the total amount of situational control.

Good work. Now try Probe 6 on page 55.

PROBE 6

A friend of yours who is an executive trainee says that it's easy to be a leader of any group if you have a lot of power to reward and punish subordinates. She says, "You give me the authority, and there's no way I won't be in control."
What do you say to her in response to this statement?

_____ a. You are right. If you have enough power, people will do what you tell them to do, and that is leadership control.

_____ b. You are wrong. What good is the ability to force people to do something if you can't figure out what they should be doing? Besides, when your subordinates don't like you, they can usually figure out some way to "do you in" regardless of how much power you have.

_____ c. You are wrong. It's not power that counts, it's personality. If your subordinates like you, you'll be successful.

Turn to the next page for feedback.

FEEDBACK

a. **You chose (a):** *If you have enough power, people will do what you tell them to do, and that is leadership control.*

> This answer is incorrect. Sometimes force can be useful for a leader, but this simplistic approach overlooks the fact that leadership is a lot more complicated than just ordering people around. Imagine being the leader of a Board of Inquiry. Could you use your power to force the members to vote your way?

Reread the section describing the three components of situational control (pages 45–49), and make another choice in Probe 6.

b. **You chose (b):** *What good is the ability to force people to do something if you can't figure out what they should be doing? Besides, when your subordinates don't like you, they can figure out some way to "do you in" regardless of how much power you have.*

> Correct. How right you are! True leadership control is certainty about what should be done and certainty that your subordinates are willing to help you do it. It is far more complicated than just being able to order people around.

Good work; continue on page 57.

c. **You chose (c):** *Wrong. It's not power that counts, it's personality. If your subordinates like you, you'll be successful.*

> This answer is not correct. Good relations with subordinates are extremely important in a leadership position, but it is an oversimplification to think that this is the whole story. The relationship between leaders and their followers involves more than just being liked. Remember the key words in our discussion are control and influence. Being a nice person might not mean that people follow your directions. Being respected and accepted by your group will give you more control and influence in your situation, but it won't help if nobody knows how to do the job, or if it means letting people do their own thing rather than doing their job.

Make another choice in Probe 6—you've missed the point!

SUMMARY

In this chapter you were introduced to the term "situational control," which describes how much control and influence you have over your leadership situation. The three components of situational control are:

1. *Leader-Member Relations:* The degree to which the group supports the leader.
2. *Task Structure:* The degree to which the task clearly spells out goals, procedures, and specific guidelines.
3. *Position Power:* The degree to which the position gives the leader the authority to reward and punish subordinates.

The next chapter describes in detail the measurement of leader-member relations.

4

LEADER-MEMBER RELATIONS

Leadership implies control and influence over others. Your control and influence obviously will be greater if you have the support and trust of your group members than if the group rejects you or gives you only half-hearted backing. Having your group's acceptance gives you considerable control: You don't have to rely on your official power or other organizational supports such as union contracts, organizational rules, or the chain of command. You also don't have to rely on your power to reward and punish because the group members are eager to follow you anyway. We speak of this personal aspect of leader control and influence as LEADER-MEMBER RELATIONS.

Leader-member relations are the MOST IMPORTANT single aspect of situational control. Good relations and support from your group assure you of either high or moderate situational control. While leaders who have good relations with their group members are not necessarily more effective, they are clearly more influential, and their group members generally are more satisfied with their jobs.

Unfortunately, it is sometimes rather difficult to tell just how much support and backing a group is likely to give you. Most of us tend to do some wishful thinking in this area—we like to believe that our relations are better than they actually are, and you must guard against thinking that the group is behind you when this is really not the case. There are a number of clues that may help you assess the extent to which subordinates accept your direction. For example:

- Do your group members try to keep you out of trouble?
- Do they warn you about potential difficulties?

- Are they conscientious about how they do their job?
- Do they do what you want them to do rather than doing no more than what you tell them to do?
- Do they include you in their small talk?
- Do they seem genuinely friendly and eager to please you?

If you can answer most of these questions with "yes," then your relations with your subordinates are probably good.

You must also keep in mind, however, that in cases of intragroup conflict, whether caused by personality clashes or by differences in values, background or language, leader-member relations are difficult to handle. You may be seen as favoring one clique over another, or you may be mistrusted by members who are from a different cultural background. However, in many organizations cultural differences are taken for granted and may only play a minor role.

Another factor to consider is the group's history. Some groups traditionally have good relations with their leaders while others by tradition or custom see their leaders as adversaries. This is true, for example, in some organizations with a long history of union-management conflict. It is also usually more difficult to step into the shoes of a well-liked and admired predecessor who is seen as having been unjustly discharged. If the leader before you was a disaster, you may find it easier to be accepted, but in some cases you may find that the members are mistrustful, and it may take longer to establish good relations.

Also important is your relationship with your own boss. If your boss supports you and works with you, group members are more likely to hold you in esteem. Moreover, if your recommendations to your boss are accepted and approved, your members will have more confidence in you as their leader.

The Leader-Member Relations scale (LMR) will help you to estimate your relations with your group. It has been designed to take all these factors into consideration.

Because leader-member relations represent the most important dimension in measuring situational control, the maximum number of scale points totals 40, or twice as much as the task structure scale and four times as much as the position power scale, which will be described in the next two chapters.

The LMR scale consists of eight questions with response choices ranging from "strongly agree" to "strongly disagree." Circle the number that best represents your opinion about each question. The scale is scored by adding the circled numbers and entering the total at the bottom of the scale.

Practice using this scale by completing the two probes on the following pages. Respond as if you are the leader of a typical group described by the probe. Completed scales are provided with the feedback for each job to let you compare your rating with ours. If your ratings fall within two or three points of those shown in the book, you are well within the acceptable range. You should be aware, however, that a short probe cannot convey the richness of leader-member relations in a real-life group. These probes are designed to give you some practice in using the scales.

PROBE 7

You are the supervisor of the office staff of a small government agency. You have been in this position for six years and your five subordinates have been with you for periods varying from six months to four years. The office runs very smoothly and there have been no complaints from the senior staff about the quality of the work. The nice thing about this group is that you can assign work and know that it will get completed on time and correctly. For this reason you feel that you do not have to supervise them closely, and it allows you to work on other aspects of your job.

You have lunch with your employees at least once a week and spend an occasional evening in their company. You have noticed, however, that there is some competition among the group and relations between them are sometimes strained. You have discussed this problem with your boss and he has indicated he will support any actions you take. So far, the situation has not gotten out of hand and it has not interfered with group productivity.

You estimate the leader-member relations of your group to be:

Good _____
Moderate _____
Poor _____

Now complete the LMR scale on the following page to see how well you have estimated.

LEADER-MEMBER RELATIONS SCALE

Circle the number which best repre-sents your response to each item.

	strongly agree	agree	neither agree nor disagree	disagree	strongly disagree
1. The people I supervise have trouble getting along with each other.	(1)	2	3	4	5
2. My subordinates are reliable and trustworthy.	5	(4)	3	2	1
3. There seems to be a friendly atmosphere among the people I supervise.	5	4	3	(2)	1
4. My subordinates always cooperate with me in getting the job done.	5	(4)	3	2	1
5. There is friction between my subordinates and myself.	1	2	3	(4)	5
6. My subordinates give me a good deal of help and support in getting the job done.	5	4	(3)	2	1
7. The people I supervise work well together in getting the job done.	5	4	3	(2)	1
8. I have good relations with the people I supervise.	5	(4)	3	2	1

Total Score   24

FEEDBACK

LEADER-MEMBER RELATIONS SCALE

Circle the number which best represents your response to each item.

	strongly agree	agree	neither agree nor disagree	disagree	strongly disagree
1. The people I supervise have trouble getting along with each other.	1	2	(3)	4	5
2. My subordinates are reliable and trustworthy.	(5)	4	3	2	1
3. There seems to be a friendly atmosphere among the people I supervise.	5	4	(3)	2	1
4. My subordinates always cooperate with me in getting the job done.	(5)	4	3	2	1
5. There is friction between my subordinates and myself.	1	2	3	4	(5)
6. My subordinates give me a good deal of help and support in getting the job done.	(5)	4	3	2	1
7. The people I supervise work well together in getting the job done.	5	4	(3)	2	1
8. I have good relations with the people I supervise.	(5)	4	3	2	1

Total Score   34

FEEDBACK

As you probably estimated, the leader-member relations in this situation were good. If you have a scale value in the vicinity of 34, you are in the right range. The fact that there is some competition between group members would mean that you should probably have answered items 1, 3, and 7 as "neither agree nor disagree." These conflicts obviously are not so acute that the employees cannot get the job done, and you wouldn't feel as confident in freeing yourself from close supervision. So choosing the answer in the middle would, most likely, represent the situation accurately. Because your relations with them are good, their occasional conflict would not effectively lower your LMR score.

A score of 30 or above on the LMR scale indicates good leader-member relations, a score of 20–30 indicates moderate leader-member relations, and a score below 20 indicates poor leader-member relations.

Try Probe 8 on the following page.

PROBE 8

You are a supervisor for the Jinglebell Telephone Company in one of the smaller rural districts. Your primary responsibility is to supervise the 22 telephone operators and 6 information operators to provide service for the community. You have recently been transferred to this district from a similar job in a major city and feel a lot of pressure from your new boss to keep things running smoothly, but you are not getting much support. In addition, most of the operators on your shift have been at their jobs for a number of years and strongly resent having an outsider brought in to replace their former boss with whom they had worked a long time.

You feel that much could be done to improve the phone service by using more modern methods. Most of your employees are unwilling to take suggestions from you regarding their phone contacts with the public. Several of the newer operators have been trying to persuade the group to cooperate and this has caused a lot of trouble and tension. Several angry arguments have occurred among the group members and between you and your staff.

You estimate your leader-member relations to be:

Good _____
Moderate _____
Poor _____

Now complete the LMR scale for this job on the following page.

LEADER-MEMBER RELATIONS SCALE

Circle the number which best represents your response to each item.

	strongly agree	agree	neither agree nor disagree	disagree	strongly disagree
1. The people I supervise have trouble getting along with each other.	1	2	3	4	5
2. My subordinates are reliable and trustworthy.	5	4	3	2	1
3. There seems to be a friendly atmosphere among the people I supervise.	5	4	3	2	1
4. My subordinates always cooperate with me in getting the job done.	5	4	3	2	1
5. There is friction between my subordinates and myself.	1	2	3	4	5
6. My subordinates give me a good deal of help and support in getting the job done.	5	4	3	2	1
7. The people I supervise work well together in getting the job done.	5	4	3	2	1
8. I have good relations with the people I supervise.	5	4	3	2	1

Total Score

FEEDBACK

LEADER-MEMBER RELATIONS SCALE

Circle the number which best represents your response to each item.

	strongly agree	agree	neither agree nor disagree	disagree	strongly disagree
1. The people I supervise have trouble getting along with each other.	(1)	2	3	4	5
2. My subordinates are reliable and trustworthy.	5	4	3	(2)	1
3. There seems to be a friendly atmosphere among the people I supervise.	5	4	3	(2)	1
4. My subordinates always cooperate with me in getting the job done.	5	4	3	(2)	1
5. There is friction between my subordinates and myself.	(1)	2	3	4	5
6. My subordinates give me a good deal of help and support in getting the job done.	5	4	3	2	(1)
7. The people I supervise work well together in getting the job done.	5	4	3	2	(1)
8. I have good relations with the people I supervise.	5	4	3	2	(1)

Total Score | *11* |

FEEDBACK

Obviously, this situation implies that you have poor leader-member relations. As you can see from the feedback scale, a total of 11 would be appropriate. However, if your score is less than 20 you got this one right.

In a situation where your employees don't support and trust you, and dissension exists among them, your control and influence over the group is going to be either low or, at best, moderate. This situation is, of course, an extreme one but it does give you an opportunity to look at the scale from a less positive viewpoint.

SUMMARY

Leaders' relations with group members are the most important single factor in determining situational control. If you have the support of your group, you can rely on group members to do their job well and willingly. This then gives you considerable control and influence even if your formal power to reward and punish is relatively slight or if your task is low in structure.

This chapter introduced the leader-member relations (LMR) scale. You should recognize that a scale of this type can be no better than your own sensitivity to group members' relations with you and with each other. For this reason, you should make it a practice to observe your group in action as often as possible and learn to assess your leader-member relations.

In particular, there are two major components you need to consider:

- The support you get from your subordinates.
- The relations among members of your group, including the dissension and conflict among them.

In the table below you will find leader-member relations scores for leaders in a number of different jobs. As we said earlier, many of us have a tendency to be overly optimistic about relations with our group members. The scores presented below reflect this tendency. The average score is approximately 32. In general, then, leaders in these different positions scored a "4" on each question.

TABLE 4–1 Average Leader-Member Relations
Scores from Different Occupational Group Samples

Job Title	LMR Score
Battalion Chiefs Urban Fire Department	29.87
National Guard Senior Officers	32.45
Administrators City Treasurer's Office	29.50
Principals Public School	32.94
Head Nurses U.S. and Canadian	21.04
Nurse Supervisors U.S.	31.36
Hotel Managers	32.57
Second Level Managers Mexico	34.55
State Executives Reporting to the Governor	34.18
Assistant State Executives	32.00
Company Commanders (U.S. Army)	32.16
Battalion Staff Officers (U.S. Army)	33.61
Captains Urban Fire Department	29.90
Lieutenants Urban Fire Department	30.98
Fire Fighters Urban Fire Department	31.27

5

MEASURING TASK STRUCTURE

The second step in determining situational control is to measure task structure. You might not have thought of the task or the nature of the job as directly affecting your control and influence. However, consider the case of a construction foreman who says to his men, "I guess they want us to build a storage shed someplace around here, so let's see what we can do."

In effect, this foreman tells his group members that he doesn't know exactly what to do and invites the crew to argue about the nature and placement of the shed. If the same foreman has a blueprint in his hand telling him exactly how to build the storage shed and where to place it, he will get no arguments from his crew.

Also, if the job, "to build a shed someplace around here" is actually completed, it may later be criticized by the foreman's boss for not being built in the right way or in the right spot. The foreman is likely to feel a little anxiety and concern about the way he builds the shed, whether it will be in the right place, and if it will fit the boss's notion of what it ought to look like. There is no such uncertainty when the blueprint specifies the location and method of building. Leaders, therefore, feel that they have more situational control if their task is highly structured and they know what is to be done.

Being told exactly what to do and how to do it relieves leaders from the uncertainty of guessing what is expected of them and what the outcome of their decisions will be. In effect, it tells the group that the supervisor knows exactly what is supposed to be done, and that he or she has the full backing of the organization for doing this work in the approved manner. The well-known military method of "doing things by the numbers" may not always be the most efficient, but it is the equivalent of the blueprint, as is standard operating procedure in business and industry. In each of these cases leaders have more control over the job being done, and their subordinates are less likely to question their authority.

A quite different situation exists in jobs where the nature of the task simply cannot be reduced to a step-by-step procedure, and where the outcome may not be known until well after the task is completed, perhaps years later. Let us take, for example, the job of a public relations director. This job is creative and involves supervising creative people. If the director is asked to design a publicity campaign, he or she will probably brainstorm with the staff to find a solution to the problem. Each member of the staff may have some good ideas as well as some that may prove worthless. There is no sure way to tell which approach will succeed and which will fail—and the outcome may not be known for months or years after the job is completed.

Likewise, the director of a research laboratory has a very unstructured task. It is extremely difficult to predict which line of research will turn into a blind alley and which will lead to success or a marketable product. Every wrong turn carries a high cost in time and money. Again, the outcome may remain uncertain for several years.

Since there are few rules to follow, there are no "best" procedures in developing a research program, and the risk of failure is high. As a result, it is hard for the research director to say to the group that he or she is right and they are wrong. The members of a research staff must constantly use their own judgment, and the director of the group cannot supervise and control every step of the project. The supervisor of a highly unstructured task can exercise only nominal control over the way the task is performed.

As we said earlier, task structure is second in importance to leader-member relations and is more difficult to measure. The measure of task structure consists of a two-part scale. Part 1 is based on aspects of task structure discussed next. Part 2 involves the effect of training and experience on task structure and will be discussed in more detail later in this chapter.

As with the Leader-Member Relations scale, this scale has been weighted to reflect its importance in measuring situational control. The maximum score possible on the task structure scale is 20, half as much as the LMR scale and twice as much as the Position Power scale discussed in the next chapter.

COMPONENTS OF TASK STRUCTURE

To measure task structure, we must consider four questions:

Is the Goal or Outcome Clearly Stated or Known?   How clearly are the requirements of your job (the tasks or duties that typically constitute your job) stated or known to you? For example, consider how your directions are given: Repair this car so that it runs again; paint this building white; or, develop a new training program; write a policy statement. The first two examples tell you exactly what is expected—the car should run; the building should look white after you get through with it. In the second set of examples, it is really up to you to guess what kind of training program will be acceptable to your boss, or exactly what the policy statement will say.

Is There Only One Way to Accomplish the Task?   If your job can be done properly only by following one or two methods, the task is more "structured" than if it could be done using a wide variety of procedures. For example, the supervisor of an axle assembly line in an auto manufacturing plant insures that workers bolt front or rear axle assemblies to a chassis. This can be done correctly in only one way. However, a job calling for improving or discovering new products might proceed in any number of ways. Therefore, the job is low in task structure.

Is There Only One Correct Answer or Solution Possible for Completing the Task?   If there is only one "correct solution" for a task, it is more highly structured than if many solutions are possible. Most bookkeeping procedures have only one correct answer; designing a building may have a large number of possible outcomes as well, for instance, the development of a short story, or designing a recruiting display.

How Easy Is It to Check Whether the Job Was Done Right?   You have to consider the degree to which it is possible to determine the "correctness" of the solution or decisions you make in the performance of your job. If you build a structure, you can check the dimensions of the building against specifications on the blueprint. If you assemble a machine, you can determine how well it performs. If you estimate the number of people who live in a district, you can check your estimate against the latest census data. These kinds of tasks are comparatively high in structure.

For some jobs, however, it is difficult to know whether the outcome was successful or unsuccessful, whether your group performed well or poorly. A group of economists may come to an agreement that a cut in taxes will create more jobs . . . "other things being equal," but it may never be possible to establish if they are right. You may be responsible for developing a new policy on job rotation for your company, but it will be difficult to determine whether the system is effective. These kinds of jobs are lower in task structure.

It also makes an important difference whether you can get feedback on the results of your work. Are there milestones and benchmarks along the way to allow you to make corrections in your course? Using them, can you see whether you are making right or wrong decisions? A builder can check whether various requirements have been met, a construction engineer can conduct stress tests; a production manager can institute various quality controls at important points in the process. All of these are highly structured tasks.

Other jobs do not provide constant feedback. The scriptwriting team working on a movie has no way to tell in advance if the audience will accept their product. If such predictions were possible, there would be few movies that fail. Or consider the general who will not know the success of the campaign plan until it is too late to do anything about it. These situations are lower in structure.

Part 1 of the Task Structure Scale is designed to reflect these aspects of task structure. It consists of ten questions with response choices of "Usually," "Sometimes," or "Seldom," and each choice is assigned a value ranging from 0 to 2. The questions are fairly straightforward and are representative of the four dimensions of task structure discussed above. However, a couple of questions may cause you some difficulty.

Question 2, for example, asks, "Is there a person available to advise and give a description of the finished product or service, or how the job should be done?" This person could be anyone from your boss to a subordinate, or someone who had the job before. The important point is not whether the person is a boss, subordinate, or fellow supervisor, but rather whether there is someone who can help clarify the job with detailed instructions.

Question 8 asks "Is there a generally agreed upon understanding about the standards the particular product or service has to meet to be considered acceptable?" For example, the standards for repairing a car require headlights to be aligned in a particular way, or water pressure to be at a certain level. The standards for training apprentices how to clean and care for a piece of machinery are clearly specified. On the other hand, planning a program to improve community relations is rather open-ended, and even where particular standards for the program are spelled out, a great deal of leeway exists. In other words, reasonable people may well arrive at quite different judgments and conclusions. It is often difficult, therefore, to tell when this kind of task has been accomplished effectively.

You may have trouble with Question 9, which relates to the previous question, and asks, "Is the evaluation of this task generally made on some quantitative basis?" In other words, can task performance be accurately rated by different people using the same objective standards of measurement? For example, the USDA meat rating system, a city plumbing code, or an aircraft inspection checklist, are all objective, quantative systems for evaluating tasks. Rating the performance of an orchestra is not dependent on such rigid criteria.

Read each question on the scale carefully and circle the number that best represents your choice. Keep in mind the various examples on the preceding pages that illustrate each of these important dimensions. If you have trouble answering a particular question, refer back to the discussion of that dimension for clarification. After completing the scale, add the circled responses and enter the total in the box marked "Subtotal." Remember that this is only the first part of the total task-structure score.

On the following pages, three jobs are to be rated on Part 1 of the Task Structure Scale. A completed scale is provided with the feedback for each job. If your ratings come out within 2 or 3 points of the score given in the feedback, you are well within the acceptable range.

PROBE 9

DIRECTOR OF PUBLIC RELATIONS OF THE MAGNUM OPUS COR-
PORATION. The director and her staff have responsibility for developing and
maintaining the company's positive image. Her team uses available information channels to reach the public with the company's story. She has the
responsibility for advising the company on the public relations impact of
various courses of action.

Estimate the task structure of the job:

High _____
Medium _____
Low _____

Now rate the job on the task structure rating scale on the following page.

TASK STRUCTURE RATING SCALE—PART 1

Circle the number in the appropriate column.	Usually True	Sometimes True	Seldom True
Is the Goal Clearly Stated or Known?			
1. Is there a blueprint, picture, model or detailed description available of the finished product or service?	2	1	0
2. Is there a person available to advise and give a description of the finished product or service, or how the job should be done?	2	1	0
Is There Only One Way to Accomplish the Task?			
3. Is there a step-by-step procedure, or a standard operating procedure which indicates in detail the process which is to be followed?	2	1	0
4. Is there a specific way to subdivide the task into separate parts or steps?	2	1	0
5. Are there some ways which are clearly recognized as better than others for performing this task?	2	1	0
Is There Only One Correct Answer or Solution?			
6. Is it obvious when the task is finished and the correct solution has been found?	2	1	0
7. Is there a book, manual, or job description which indicates the best solution or the best outcome for the task?	2	1	0
Is It Easy to Check Whether the Job Was Done Right?			
8. Is there a generally agreed upon understanding about the standards the particular product or service has to meet to be considered acceptable?	2	1	0
9. Is the evaluation of this task generally made on some quantitative basis?	2	1	0
10. Can the leader and the group find out how well the task has been accomplished in enough time to improve future performance?	2	1	0

SUBTOTAL _____

FEEDBACK

TASK STRUCTURE RATING SCALE—PART 1

Circle the number in the appropriate column.	Usually True	Sometimes True	Seldom True
Is the Goal Clearly Stated or Known?			
1. Is there a blueprint, picture, model or detailed description available of the finished product or service?	2	1	(0)
2. Is there a person available to advise and give a description of the finished product or service, or how the job should be done?	2	(1)	0
Is There Only One Way to Accomplish the Task?			
3. Is there a step-by-step procedure, or a standard operating procedure which indicates in detail the process which is to be followed?	2	1	(0)
4. Is there a specific way to subdivide the task into separate parts or steps?	2	1	(0)
5. Are there some ways which are clearly recognized as better than others for performing this task?	2	(1)	0
Is There Only One Correct Answer or Solution?			
6. Is it obvious when the task is finished and the correct solution has been found?	2	1	(0)
7. Is there a book, manual, or job description which indicates the best solution or the best outcome for the task?	2	1	(0)
Is It Easy to Check Whether the Job Was Done Right?			
8. Is there a generally agreed upon understanding about the standards the particular product or service has to meet to be considered acceptable?	2	(1)	0
9. Is the evaluation of this task generally made on some quantitative basis?	2	1	(0)
10. Can the leader and the group find out how well the task has been accomplished in enough time to improve future performance?	2	1	(0)

SUBTOTAL ___*3*___

FEEDBACK

The job of Public Relations Director would receive a score of about 3 on the task structure scale. This would mean the job is low in task structure. A score of 6 or below is low in structure, a score between 7 and 13 is medium in structure, and a score of 14 or above is high in task structure.

The total number of points possible is 20. As with the leader-member relations scale in the previous chapter, this scale has been weighted to reflect its importance in determining situational control. Since task structure is second in importance to leader-member relations, it is worth half the number of points.

How well were you able to estimate the structure of this job? The Public Relations Director's job is very low in structure since there is no clear way to maintain a public image. There are no guidelines, blueprints, or detailed directions. There are many ways to accomplish the task and it is hard to check whether the job was done right.

Question 2 should have been answered with "sometimes" since the director probably has a superior who could give detailed advice.

Question 5 was worth one point since "sometimes" there are ways to proceed which are recognized as better than others.

Question 8 was also worth one point since it is generally understood that the job is done right as long as the company image stays high.

The rest of the questions should have been answered with "seldom." If you came up with a score within 2 or 3 points of the suggested score, you are catching on. If you missed this one, go back to pages 73–77 and review the discussion of task structure. Then try the next probe and see how well you do.

PROBE 10

SERVICE MANAGER IN CHARGE OF MOTOR POOL MAINTENANCE FOR THE MUDDY TRAILS BUS LINES. The job requires that vehicles be kept in running order and available for authorized use. In addition, routine scheduled maintenance must be carried out. This includes such procedures as oil changes, filter changes, and lubrication.

Estimate the task structure of this job:

High _____
Medium _____
Low _____

Complete the task structure scale on the following page.

TASK STRUCTURE RATING SCALE—PART 1

Circle the number in the appropriate column.	Usually True	Sometimes True	Seldom True
Is the Goal Clearly Stated or Known?			
1. Is there a blueprint, picture, model or detailed description available of the finished product or service?	2	1	0
2. Is there a person available to advise and give a description of the finished product or service, or how the job should be done?	2	1	0
Is There Only One Way to Accomplish the Task?			
3. Is there a step-by-step procedure, or a standard operating procedure which indicates in detail the process which is to be followed?	2	1	0
4. Is there a specific way to subdivide the task into separate parts or steps?	2	1	0
5. Are there some ways which are clearly recognized as better than others for performing this task?	2	1	0
Is There Only One Correct Answer or Solution?			
6. Is it obvious when the task is finished and the correct solution has been found?	2	1	0
7. Is there a book, manual, or job description which indicates the best solution or the best outcome for the task?	2	1	0
Is It Easy to Check Whether the Job Was Done Right?			
8. Is there a generally agreed upon understanding about the standards the particular product or service has to meet to be considered acceptable?	2	1	0
9. Is the evaluation of this task generally made on some quantitative basis?	2	1	0
10. Can the leader and the group find out how well the task has been accomplished in enough time to improve future performance?	2	1	0

SUBTOTAL _____

FEEDBACK

TASK STRUCTURE RATING SCALE—PART 1

Circle the number in the appropriate column.	Usually True	Sometimes True	Seldom True

Is the Goal Clearly Stated or Known?

	Usually True	Sometimes True	Seldom True
1. Is there a blueprint, picture, model or detailed description available of the finished product or service?	②	1	0
2. Is there a person available to advise and give a description of the finished product or service, or how the job should be done?	②	1	0

Is There Only One Way to Accomplish the Task?

3. Is there a step-by-step procedure, or a standard operating procedure which indicates in detail the process which is to be followed?	②	1	0
4. Is there a specific way to subdivide the task into separate parts or steps?	②	1	0
5. Are there some ways which are clearly recognized as better than others for performing this task?	②	1	0

Is There Only One Correct Answer or Solution?

6. Is it obvious when the task is finished and the correct solution has been found?	②	1	0
7. Is there a book, manual, or job description which indicates the best solution or the best outcome for the task?	②	1	0

Is It Easy to Check Whether the Job Was Done Right?

8. Is there a generally agreed upon understanding about the standards the particular product or service has to meet to be considered acceptable?	②	1	0
9. Is the evaluation of this task generally made on some quantitative basis?	②	1	0
10. Can the leader and the group find out how well the task has been accomplished in enough time to improve future performance?	②	1	0

SUBTOTAL ____ *20*

FEEDBACK

If you estimated this job as high in task structure, you are doing well. A score of 14 or above indicates that the job is high in structure, and this one scored 20. Compare this with your rating and see how close you came.

This job is so highly structured that it received the most points for every question. If you came close to 20 you are doing well and should move on to Probe 11 on the next page. If you are still having trouble, you should review this chapter before trying Probe 11.

PROBE 11

PLANT SECURITY CHIEF. Duties include supervision of 20 to 30 security personnel; planning, directing, and supervising all phases of plant security. Meets with administrative staff and local law enforcement agencies regarding mutual problems; provides assistance upon request. Develops training programs to provide a competent security staff; schedules their supervisory shift assignments; hires personnel. Investigates complaints and reports violations of plant security regulations. Must be prepared and alert for any extraordinary or emergency situations involving plant security.

Estimate the task structure of this job:

High _____
Medium _____
Low _____

Now rate this job on the task structure rating scale on the following page.

TASK STRUCTURE RATING SCALE—PART 1

Circle the number in the appropriate column.	Usually True	Sometimes True	Seldom True
Is the Goal Clearly Stated or Known?			
1. Is there a blueprint, picture, model or detailed description available of the finished product or service?	2	1	0
2. Is there a person available to advise and give a description of the finished product or service, or how the job should be done?	2	1	0
Is There Only One Way to Accomplish the Task?			
3. Is there a step-by-step procedure, or a standard operating procedure which indicates in detail the process which is to be followed?	2	1	0
4. Is there a specific way to subdivide the task into separate parts or steps?	2	1	0
5. Are there some ways which are clearly recognized as better than others for performing this task?	2	1	0
Is There Only One Correct Answer or Solution?			
6. Is it obvious when the task is finished and the correct solution has been found?	2	1	0
7. Is there a book, manual, or job description which indicates the best solution or the best outcome for the task?	2	1	0
Is It Easy to Check Whether the Job Was Done Right?			
8. Is there a generally agreed upon understanding about the standards the particular product or service has to meet to be considered acceptable?	2	1	0
9. Is the evaluation of this task generally made on some quantitative basis?	2	1	0
10. Can the leader and the group find out how well the task has been accomplished in enough time to improve future performance?	2	1	0

SUBTOTAL _____

FEEDBACK

TASK STRUCTURE RATING SCALE—PART 1

Circle the number in the appropriate column.	Usually True	Sometimes True	Seldom True
Is the Goal Clearly Stated or Known?			
1. Is there a blueprint, picture, model or detailed description available of the finished product or service?	2	1	(0)
2. Is there a person available to advise and give a description of the finished product or service, or how the job should be done?	(2)	1	0
Is There Only One Way to Accomplish the Task?			
3. Is there a step-by-step procedure, or a standard operating procedure which indicates in detail the process which is to be followed?	2	(1)	0
4. Is there a specific way to subdivide the task into separate parts or steps?	(2)	1	0
5. Are there some ways which are clearly recognized as better than others for performing this task?	(2)	1	0
Is There Only One Correct Answer or Solution?			
6. Is it obvious when the task is finished and the correct solution has been found?	2	(1)	0
7. Is there a book, manual, or job description which indicates the best solution or the best outcome for the task?	2	(1)	0
Is It Easy to Check Whether the Job Was Done Right?			
8. Is there a generally agreed upon understanding about the standards the particular product or service has to meet to be considered acceptable?	2	(1)	0
9. Is the evaluation of this task generally made on some quantitative basis?	2	1	(0)
10. Can the leader and the group find out how well the task has been accomplished in enough time to improve future performance?	2	(1)	0

SUBTOTAL ___11___

FEEDBACK

The plant security chief job occupies a middle point on the task structure dimension. The correct score is around 11. As long as your total score is between 7 and 13, even if you emphasized somewhat different aspects, you are doing well.

Some of the chief's duties are quite clear and covered by rules and guidelines. The highest number of points was awarded for questions 4 and 5. Question 2 also scored highly since the security officer would have a plant manager to turn to for advice and assistance. Some of his duties, however, require making decisions and using his own judgment; therefore, "sometimes" is probably the better answer for questions 3, 6, 7, 8, and 10. Question 1 received no points since there really isn't a blueprint, picture, or model of the finished product, and question 9 received 0 since there is no quantitative basis for measuring how well the job is done.

The security chief's job contains some routine aspects (e.g., patrolling the grounds, setting schedules, filling out payroll forms) and some less structured activities (guarding against theft, industrial sabotage or espionage, internal pilfering). The combination of the routine and nonroutine portions of the job place it in the midrange on task structure.

If your ratings on these three probes don't come close to those shown in the feedback, review pages 73–77 of this chapter before continuing.

If your scores are in the ballpark you are ready to continue on to Part 2 of the scale on the effects of training and experience on task structure, introduced on the next page.

EFFECTS OF LEADERSHIP EXPERIENCE AND TRAINING ON TASK STRUCTURE

Without adequate leadership training and experience, a leader's task structure is necessarily lower. Therefore, we must adjust the task structure score to reflect lack of experience and training.

Experience and Task Structure

When we speak of leaders with adequate experience, we mean that they have held leadership positions long enough to learn how to cope with most of the problems usually confronting people in a leadership position. Experience is on-the-job training, and it usually goes along with some coaching by others who are involved with the leader. New leaders are likely to get hints from their superiors, from the person who was in the job before them, and from others in similar positions. They are also likely to get some guidance from the people they supervise. They will be told, for example, that "we always did it this way before," or "you'll find that Method A works better."

The highly experienced leader will have faced the same problem time and time again: The work sheets didn't get filled in today, three of the eight people in the department are sick again, Sam and Mike got into an argument over who made the mistake on the last job, and Walt, the new man, is giving you a lot of lip every time he's told to do something.

Experience teaches leaders how to handle these problems. They will no longer get flustered because they've been through all this before. They will know that a call to the payroll department will take care of the time sheet problem, that the way to handle Walt is to ignore him, while they need to talk to Sam and Mike like a Dutch uncle.

What this means is that experience has made the total situation more predictable and less uncertain. The job will seem more structured as time goes by and require fewer new solutions since fewer brand new problems arise. In other words, experience has made the leadership situation more secure, less anxiety arousing, and consequently, it has given the leader more control over the outcome.

Effects of Training on Task Structure

Leadership training and experience often are closely related. Most good training tries to reflect the experience of others in integrated and easily digested form. Its main purpose is to make it unnecessary for trainees to figure everything out for themselves. They learn from others what has and has not been effective. By teaching them what has worked for others and letting them practice how to handle various situations, we are in effect trying to make the job more structured. There is less ambiguity about how to perform a task. More guidelines are suggested for telling whether things are proceeding in the right way (easier evaluation) and a better understanding of what is to be accomplished (more goal clarity). Most technical training will make leaders more competent and, therefore, more knowledgeable in their job. They will, therefore, have more control.

A course of training may also "unfreeze" some previous ideas. It may show leaders alternative ways of doing their job or prepare them to handle complications specific to the new job. Leaders who have performed well in the past may learn through training that they have overlooked or ignored a number of aspects in their leadership situation. For example, they may have ignored the feelings of their subordinates and may have to pay more attention to interpersonal relations with coworkers. However, training usually makes tasks more structured and gives more control.

DOES EXPERIENCE AND TRAINING STRUCTURE SOME TASKS MORE THAN OTHERS?

Some tasks and jobs can be greatly improved by training or by experience. Others do not benefit from either doing the same job over and over, or from getting specific instructions on how to do the job. No matter how much we might train an individual to become an inventor, being inventive is a personal attribute that might be assisted but cannot be taught. Likewise, it is difficult to teach anyone how to be a brilliant conductor of an orchestra, although it is possible to teach the fundamentals of conducting.

Other types of tasks can be readily taught. Generally speaking, the more structured tasks can be taught more easily than highly unstructured tasks. It is relatively easy to teach an individual how to march men around on a drill field, or how to direct an assembly operation. It is difficult to teach someone how to direct a play or manage a political campaign.

The less structured the task, the more judgment is required, and the task becomes more dependent on the leader's creativity or ability to encourage creativity in others. Unstructured tasks, therefore, are less easily improved by training, and the leader will be less likely to benefit from the experience of others.

Most training, particularly technical training, is a method used to make tasks more structured: It provides rules and routines that trainees otherwise might not know, and presents methods to assist them in doing the job without having to create or invent new methods for themselves. However, even a highly structured task will seem relatively unstructured without adequate training.

A good example is provided by trying to follow a recipe for making a soufflé. Although recipes are proverbially clear and give step-by-step instructions, the novice will still have many baffling questions—e.g., how does one fold an egg? Similar problems are invariably encountered by any novice who tackles the "easy-to-follow" instructions on programming a computer.

MEASURING THE EFFECTS OF TRAINING AND EXPERIENCE

Insofar as training and experience affect task structure, we must adjust our score to reflect this factor. The task structure ratings you read about in the first part of this chapter are based on the assumption that the leader has had adequate experience and/or training appropriate for the task.

If leaders do not have adequate training and experience, we must *subtract* points from the task structure score, since the task will be less structured for the inexperienced or untrained leader than for the "old hand." An additional scale is therefore needed. This scale contains only two items. These are to be answered either for yourself, in a leadership position, or for another leader whom you are describing:

a. Compared to others in this or similar positions, how much training has the leader had?

3	2	1	0
Full training	Very little training	Moderate amount	No training at all

b. Compared to others in this or similar positions, how much experience has the leader had?

6	4	2	0
No experience	Very little experience	Moderate amount of experience	A great deal of experience

As we have already said, jobs with very low structure do not benefit greatly by experience and training. Therefore:

MAKE NO ADJUSTMENT FOR JOBS WITH SCORES BELOW 6 ON PART 1 FOR EXPERIENCE AND TRAINING.

Note that we are talking here about RELEVANT training and experience. Thus, if you are promoted to sales manager, training in special sales techniques or advertising would be relevant. Training in typing would not be relevant. Experience that is related to the present job, even if indirectly, should be counted.

It is not possible to determine for every leadership position what specific training or experience is important. You must use your knowledge of each unique situation in making these ratings. Most leaders know enough about their own jobs and the jobs of their subordinates to do this.

A good rule of thumb is the following:

- If your coworkers or superiors frequently seek you out for advice or assistance on difficult jobs, the chances are that you have had a great deal of experience and/or training.
- If you often need to consult others on how your job is to be done, or on various problems you encounter, the chances are that you have had very little training and/or experience.
- If you are neither asked for assistance and advice, nor need to ask others, you are probably average in training and experience.

To illustrate the effects of training and experience, let's examine the probe we just completed on the plant security chief. In this probe we described and rated the job of a security officer. The position came out as moderate in task structure (score-11). Suppose, however, we now know that the particular man in this position had very little training, perhaps a couple of short courses in security methods and procedures. We also know that he has been on this job for only four months, which is very little compared to other people in the field.

His task structure rating scale would now look like the one on the following pages. One other point—a leader's experience not only affects task structure but situational control in general. In some jobs, leadership experience may be very important in determining situational control. This is the case, for example, in such organizations as the military in which a leader has to know a host of unwritten rules and customs. You will obviously have to use some judgment in deciding how much difference experience makes in determining your overall situational control. We will come back to this problem in Chapter 9.

As you can see from the example illustrated on the following scale, the previously moderate task structure rating of the security chief is now low because of the chief's lack of training and experience. Again, DO NOT make a training and experience adjustment if the Part 1 score is lower than 6.

TASK STRUCTURE RATING SCALE—PART 1

Circle the number in the appropriate column.	Usually True	Sometimes True	Seldom True
Is the Goal Clearly Stated or Known?			
1. Is there a blueprint, picture, model or detailed description available of the finished product or service?	2	1	(0)
2. Is there a person available to advise and give a description of the finished product or service, or how the job should be done?	(2)	1	0
Is There Only One Way to Accomplish the Task?			
3. Is there a step-by-step procedure, or a standard operating procedure which indicates in detail the process which is to be followed?	2	(1)	0
4. Is there a specific way to subdivide the task into separate parts or steps?	(2)	1	0
5. Are there some ways which are clearly recognized as better than others for performing this task?	(2)	1	0
Is There Only One Correct Answer or Solution?			
6. Is it obvious when the task is finished and the correct solution has been found?	2	(1)	0
7. Is there a book, manual, or job description which indicates the best solution or the best outcome for the task?	2	(1)	0
Is It Easy to Check Whether the Job Was Done Right?			
8. Is there a generally agreed upon understanding about the standards the particular product or service has to meet to be considered acceptable?	2	(1)	0
9. Is the evaluation of this task generally made on some quantitative basis?	2	1	(0)
10. Can the leader and the group find out how well the task has been accomplished in enough time to improve future performance?	2	(1)	0

SUBTOTAL ___11___

TASK STRUCTURE RATING SCALE—PART 2

Training and Experience Adjustment

NOTE: Do not adjust jobs with task structure scores of 6 or below.

a. Compared to others in this or similar positions, how much *training* has the leader had?

3	②	1	0
No training at all	Very little training	A moderate amount of training	A great deal of training

b. Compared to others in this or similar positions, how much *experience* has the leader had?

6	④	2	0
No experience at all	Very little experience	A moderate amount of experience	A great deal of experience

Add lines (a) and (b) of the training and experience adjustment, then *subtract* this from the subtotal given in Part 1.

Subtotal from Part 1. $\boxed{11}$

Subtract training and experience adjustment $\boxed{-6}$

Total Task Structure Score $\boxed{5}$

SUMMARY

Task structure means the degree to which procedures, goals, and evaluation of a task can be defined. The leader who is given a highly structured task enjoys considerably more influence and control than one who is given a very unstructured task. The structured task, typified by work done on an assembly line, according to a blueprint, or a standard operating procedure gives members of a work unit little reason or opportunity to challenge the leader's decisions, and it provides the leader with a great deal of assurance that the job can be accomplished as long as the task is done in accordance with specifications and the organization's procedures.

We measure task structure on the basis of four related questions:

1. Is the goal or outcome clearly stated or known?
2. Is there only one way to accomplish the task or are there innumerable methods which might be used to accomplish the goal?
3. Is there only one correct answer or solution, or many possible solutions to the problem or ways of performing the task?
4. Is it easy to check whether the job was done right, or is it difficult to evaluate the outcome of the task?

Training and experience tend to increase the structure of the task for the leader. Therefore, when we examine task structure we must take into account the amount of training and experience the leader has had.

Below are listed average task structure scores for leaders in a variety of jobs both foreign and domestic. You will notice subtle score differences between jobs, just as you would expect.

Table 5–1   Task Structure Scores for Various Occupational Groups

Job Title	Task Structure Score
Hotel Managers	15.88
Head Nurses U.S. and Canadian	14.61
Second Level Managers Mexico	13.98
Company Commanders U.S. Army	12.46
Battalion Staff Officers U.S. Army	12.38
Fire Fighters Urban Fire Department	11.54
Principals Public School	10.86
National Guard Senior Officers	9.5
Lieutenants Urban Fire Department	9.37
Captains Urban Fire Department	8.25
Battalion Chief Urban Fire Department	8.13
Administrators City Treasurer's Office	7.75
Assistant State Executives	6.36
State Executives Reporting to the Governor	6.35
Nurse Supervisors U.S.	6.15

6

MEASURING POSITION POWER

The final step in measuring situational control is to determine the amount of position power given to a leader. One obvious way in which an organization "gives" a leader power is by assigning him or her to a position having certain rights, duties, and obligations. These usually include the use of rewards and punishments to enforce legitimate orders and directives.

Leadership positions vary, of course, in how much formal power they confer on their occupants. In some cases, the leader can hire and fire at will, assign tasks or transfer a subordinate from one job to another, from one department to another, and even from one city to another. Other organizations severely limit what the leader may or may not do. He or she may only be allowed to give verbal reprimands, or recommend such penalties as demotion, fines, or suspension. Official rewards may include giving pay raises, extra vacation days, time off, or more informally, giving a subordinate desirable job assignments.

At one extreme are leadership positions in which the leader has enormous power; at the other are positions in which the leader has practically no official power to punish or reward. For instance, the chairperson of a volunteer committee can only try and persuade or cajole other members, or praise them when they do a good job.

No matter what the organization does or does not allow, almost all leaders have the implicit right to praise or to give subordinates a "chewing out," to "lean on people," or to pat them on the back. Most positions permit the leader to assign tasks and decide who will work with whom.

Remember, however, that power and authority are not simply "given" to the leader. No leader has absolute authority, and all authority and power derives from the willingness of subordinates to accept the leader's right to lead. Not even in the military services, which give a great deal of formal position power, is the leader independent of subordinates.

There is truth in the old Army adage that "You can't make a man obey an order, but you can make him sorry that he didn't." But if too many people will not obey a leader's orders willingly, the leader will not keep the position long. Most leadership, if not all, is an implied social contract. Subordinates usually will do what they are asked because this will give them various rewards and satisfactions. When leaders behave in an arbitrary manner, they are likely to lose the support of subordinates. As a result, the system breaks down, the group dissolves, or the leader is replaced. Practically all leadership power is, therefore, exercised by common consent.

This is so even in an authoritarian system like the army. We know of one case in World War II when the "Austrian Battalion" was disbanded because the leadership of the battalion did not make enough effort to be accepted by the soldiers of that unit.

Problems arise when subordinates consider rules and regulations to be unreasonable or unfairly applied. This reaffirms that the leader's power and authority derive in large part from the consent and support of subordinates and that power and authority cannot simply be "given" to somebody in a leadership position.

Also important is the backing and support of leaders by their superiors. If leaders recommend a reward, an administrative change, or a particular punishment, and their recommendation is refused by their superior, then their power over their own subordinates is considerably diminished.

One of the things making leadership such a difficult job is the fine line that you, as the leader, must walk between maintaining your group members' support and the demands of the organization. The organization may demand more output, but the employees may want to work at a more comfortable pace. It is your job to use your authority and position power to reach some acceptable compromise between the organization's demands and your subordinates' willingness to comply.

The position power rating scale consists of five questions about the power which the leader has at his or her disposal for directing the behavior of followers. You should be able to answer these questions from your knowledge of the kinds of privileges the organization gives you.

Some of these questions require judgment about the likely amount of power a leader might have in a particular situation. In filling out your own position scale, you must remember that people generally tend to underestimate the power of their own position and overestimate the power of others. Most of us feel that we never have as much power as we need. Be sure to guard against this tendency.

Try your hand at the probes on the following pages. Remember to imagine yourself in the role of the leader in responding to these situations.

PROBE 12

Estimate the Position Power of a Captain of a naval vessel.

    High _____

    Medium _____

    Low _____

Now rate this job on the Position Power Rating scale and compare your ratings with those provided in the feedback.

POSITION POWER RATING SCALE

Circle the number which best represents your answer.

1. Can the leader directly or by recommendation administer rewards and punishments to subordinates?

2	1	0
Can act directly or can recommend with high effectiveness	Can recommend but with mixed results	No

2. Can the leader directly or by recommendation affect the promotion, demotion, hiring, or firing of subordinates?

2	1	0
Can act directly or can recommend with high effectiveness	Can recommend but with mixed results	No

3. Does the leader have the knowledge necessary to assign tasks to subordinates and instruct them in task completion?

2	1	0
Yes	Sometimes or in some aspects	No

4. Is it the leader's job to evaluate the performance of subordinates?

2	1	0
Yes	Sometimes or in some aspects	No

5. Has the leader been given some official title of authority by the organization (e.g., foreman, department head, platoon leader)?

2	0
Yes	No

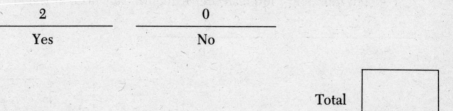

Total

FEEDBACK

POSITION POWER RATING SCALE

Circle the number which best represents your answer.

1. Can the leader directly or by recommendation administer rewards and punishments to subordinates?

②	1	0
Can act directly or can recommend with high effectiveness	Can recommend but with mixed results	No

2. Can the leader directly or by recommendation affect the promotion, demotion, hiring, or firing of subordinates?

②	1	0
Can act directly or can recommend with high effectiveness	Can recommend but with mixed results	No

3. Does the leader have the knowledge necessary to assign tasks to subordinates and instruct them in task completion?

②	1	0
Yes	Sometimes or in some aspects	No

4. Is it the leader's job to evaluate the performance of subordinates?

②	1	0
Yes	Sometimes or in some aspects	No

5. Has the leader been given some official title of authority by the organization (e.g., foreman, department head, platoon leader)?

②	0
Yes	No

Total | 10 |

FEEDBACK

This was an obvious question. The captain of a ship has one of the most powerful positions that exists.

The position should have received the maximum number of points, 10. If you awarded this position anything over 7, you were still within range and should feel comfortable continuing on to the next probe. A score of 7–10 indicates high position power; a score of 4–6 shows moderate position power and a score of 3 or below denotes low position power.

Because position power has emerged in our studies as the least important of these three dimensions, the total points you can get on the position power scale are lower than those of the other two scales. The highest score possible on position power is 10, the highest score on task structure is 20, and the highest leader-member relations score is 40.

If you missed this one, reread pages 99–101 before continuing.

PROBE 13

You have been appointed as the administrator of your company's research laboratory. You are assigned to coordinate and facilitate the research activities of a team of chemists, although you are not a chemist yourself.

This assignment requires you to provide support for the research team's activities and to assure that important organizational and scientific procedures are followed. Your major responsibilities are to disburse already allocated funds, monitor progress toward goals, and to assign projects to available research teams. You supervise the nonresearch aspects of the laboratory (e.g. proper invoice procedures, report filing, use of equipment), but do not direct the research program.

You are occasionally asked to report on individual team members, but your reports make up only a part of the members' overall evaluation. Your recommendations are not weighted very strongly; the major evaluations are made by the team leaders who direct the work of the team. Since you have many other responsibilities, you are not asked to evaluate the scientific work of the group.

Your position power is likely to be:

High _____
Moderate _____
Low _____

Now rate this job on the Position Power Rating scale and compare your ratings with those provided in the feedback.

POSITION POWER RATING SCALE

Circle the number which best represents your answer.

1. Can the leader directly or by recommendation administer rewards and punishments to subordinates?

2	1	0
Can act directly or can recommend with high effectiveness	Can recommend but with mixed results	No

2. Can the leader directly or by recommendation affect the promotion, demotion, hiring, or firing of subordinates?

2	1	0
Can act directly or can recommend with high effectiveness	Can recommend but with mixed results	No

3. Does the leader have the knowledge necessary to assign tasks to subordinates and instruct them in task completion?

2	1	0
Yes	Sometimes or in some aspects	No

4. Is it the leader's job to evaluate the performance of subordinates?

2	1	0
Yes	Sometimes or in some aspects	No

5. Has the leader been given some official title of authority by the organization (e.g., foreman, department head, platoon leader)?

2	0
Yes	No

Total

FEEDBACK

POSITION POWER RATING SCALE

Circle the number which best represents your answer.

1. Can the leader directly or by recommendation administer rewards and punishments to subordinates?

2	1	(0)
Can act directly or can recommend with high effectiveness	Can recommend but with mixed results	No

2. Can the leader directly or by recommendation affect the promotion, demotion, hiring, or firing of subordinates?

2	1	(0)
Can act directly or can recommend with high effectiveness	Can recommend but with mixed results	No

3. Does the leader have the knowledge necessary to assign tasks to subordinates and instruct them in task completion?

2	(1)	0
Yes	Sometimes or in some aspects	No

4. Is it the leader's job to evaluate the performance of subordinates?

2	(1)	0
Yes	Sometimes or in some aspects	No

5. Has the leader been given some official title of authority by the organization (e.g., foreman, department head, platoon leader)?

(2)	0
Yes	No

Total 4

FEEDBACK

This position has moderate position power. The administrator does have certain areas of authority and an official position. However, lack of expertise (and consequently, responsibility) keeps the administrator from having much of an impact on the work of team members.

The leader does, however, have an official title (so score 2 points for question 5), occasionally evaluates team member performance as PART of an overall evaluation, and makes job assignments. Therefore, questions 3 and 4 should be given a score of 1.

A total of 4 is appropriate. If you had trouble with this probe, review pages 99–101 before continuing.

PROBE 14

You are the assistant production manager in a paper products corporation. A scuffle has occurred in the sealing assembly line and one man has broken his wrist. The Director of Production wishes to undertake an investigation immediately. He has appointed a board of inquiry of three supervisors and a union official to look into the matter. Because of your position, you have been asked to chair this unofficial inquiry. You have eight hours to file a report.

Your position power is:

High _____
Medium _____
Low _____

Now rate the job on the position rating scale.

POSITION POWER RATING SCALE

Circle the number which best represents your answer.

1. Can the leader directly or by recommendation administer rewards and punishments to subordinates?

2	1	0
Can act directly or can recommend with high effectiveness	Can recommend but with mixed results	No

2. Can the leader directly or by recommendation affect the promotion, demotion, hiring, or firing of subordinates?

2	1	0
Can act directly or can recommend with high effectiveness	Can recommend but with mixed results	No

3. Does the leader have the knowledge necessary to assign tasks to subordinates and instruct them in task completion?

2	1	0
Yes	Sometimes or in some aspects	No

4. Is it the leader's job to evaluate the performance of subordinates?

2	1	0
Yes	Sometimes or in some aspects	No

5. Has the leader been given some official title of authority by the organization (e.g., foreman, department head, platoon leader)?

2	0
Yes	No

Total [ ]

FEEDBACK

POSITION POWER RATING SCALE

Circle the number which best represents your answer.

1. Can the leader directly or by recommendation administer rewards and punishments to subordinates?

2	1	(0)
Can act directly or can recommend with high effectiveness	Can recommend but with mixed results	No

2. Can the leader directly or by recommendation affect the promotion, demotion, hiring, or firing of subordinates?

2	1	(0)
Can act directly or can recommend with high effectiveness	Can recommend but with mixed results	No

3. Does the leader have the knowledge necessary to assign tasks to subordinates and instruct them in task completion?

2	(1)	0
Yes	Sometimes or in some aspects	No

4. Is it the leader's job to evaluate the performance of subordinates?

2	1	(0)
Yes	Sometimes or in some aspects	No

5. Has the leader been given some official title of authority by the organization (e.g., foreman, department head, platoon leader)?

(2)	0
Yes	No

Total 3

FEEDBACK

You clearly have low position power—a score of 3. You will be chairing a committee, and this drastically reduces your power over your subordinates—namely, THE OTHER MEMBERS OF THIS BOARD. You will not be expected to punish or reward your fellow board members.

If you are having difficulty with the position power scale, be sure and review the chapter.

SUMMARY

Position power means the authority and control a person has by virtue of occupying a particular leadership position. It includes the means leaders have at their disposal for assuring that legitimate orders and directions are carried out. These include such methods of punishment as reprimanding, scolding, docking, demoting, or, in the last resort, firing a subordinate. They may include such rewards as promotion, raises, praise, or recommending raises or promotions, as well as giving desirable assignments.

While power is officially conferred by the organization, the power of leaders is derived from their subordinates' willingness to accept the leader's authority.

The power of leaders is also affected by the support they get from their superiors. If their recommendations are generally followed, then their power will appear greater in the eyes of subordinates.

Below are position power ratings given by the leaders we have discussed in conjunction with LPC, leader-member relations, and task structure scores. The scores do not vary as much from job to job as one might expect. But you will notice that many of these jobs are quite powerful. The lowest average score was found for the job of fire fighter, which has moderate power. None of the jobs represented here have low power.

TABLE 6–1 Position Power Scores Obtained from Various Occupational Group Samples

Job Title	Position Power Score
Head Nurses U.S. and Canadian	9.48
Second Level Managers Mexico	9.46
National Guard Senior Officers	9.2
Hotel Managers	9.03
Company Commanders U.S. Army	8.83
State Executives Reporting to the Governor	8.79
Assistant State Executives	8.38
Battalion Chiefs Urban Fire Department	8.25
Principals Public School	8.08
Captains Urban Fire Department	8.05
Lieutenants Urban Fire Department	8.0
Battalion Staff Officers U.S. Army	7.92
Fire Fighters Urban Fire Department	6.6

7

COMPUTING SITUATIONAL CONTROL

The previous chapters introduced the three major factors that affect the leader's control of a situation and gave you practice in rating various jobs. The combined situational control score is obtained by simply adding the scores for the three scales. A score will fall into either the high, moderate, or low control zone. On the following page is the scale used to combine the three factors.

SITUATIONAL CONTROL SCALE

Enter the total scores for the Leader-Member Relations dimension, the Task Structure scale, and the Position Power scale in the spaces below. Add the three scores together and compare your total with the ranges given in the table below to determine your overall situational control.

1. *Leader-Member Relations Total*

2. *Task Structure Total*

3. *Position Power Total*

Grand Total

Total Score	51 – 70	31 – 50	10 – 30
Amount of Situational Control	High Control	Moderate Control	Low Control

After you have worked with this system for awhile you should be able to estimate quite accurately whether a situation is high, moderate, or low in situational control without having to complete each of the separate scales. You will, of course, have to remember that leader-member relations are about twice as important as task structure, and about four times as important as position power.

A moderate control situation will either have moderate leader-member relations, task structure, and position power, or it will be high on one or two of these and low or moderate on the others. For example, good leader-member relations, low task structure, and low position power would fall into a moderate situation as would poor leader-member relations, high task structure, and high position power.

You may wish to review the leader-member relations, task structure, and position power scores from leaders in a variety of positions that have been tabled in Chapters 4, 5, and 6. Reviewing these scores may help you more accurately estimate the situational control of your own job and those of your subordinates.

To obtain practice making estimates of situational control, complete the probes on the following pages. After you have made your estimate, fill out the scales and compare the scale values with your estimate. This will very quickly teach you to make accurate estimates without having to compute each of the scores.

PROBE 15

A dogfood company is looking for a person to supervise their shipping docks and you have decided to apply for the job. The shipping supervisor keeps track of invoices and fills and ships orders. He directs the work of various clerks and stockhandlers to see that orders are promptly filled and shipped to customers. The supervisor is also responsible for making sure that incoming raw material is properly received and routed to the right departments.

The company is doing well and morale is good. This work group has been together for a long time and has always worked well together. There has been little evidence of dissension. In fact, the members have organized a bowling team and have been bowling one night a week, and their families occasionally socialize.

Relations with management have been traditionally excellent in this department. Prior to starting the job, you will be given an intensive training course in the company's shipping procedures, although you feel you have had adequate experience in a shipping department in a previous job.

The shipping and receiving procedures are highly standardized, as is the paper work. The shipping supervisor is a first-level manager with the same rank as that of a foreman. As such, the supervisor is expected to maintain discipline and company standards, make job assignments, and evaluate employee performance at regular intervals. While the supervisor does not hire and fire, his recommendations are given considerable weight.

What is your estimate of situational control for this job?

High control _____
Moderate control _____
Low control _____

On the following pages complete the leader-member relations, task structure, and position power scales for the shipping supervisor's position. Then rate the situational control and compare these ratings with the estimate you made above. Look at the feedback and see how close you came to the ratings we provided.

LEADER-MEMBER RELATIONS SCALE

Circle the number which best repre-
sents your response to each item.

	strongly agree	agree	neither agree nor disagree	disagree	strongly disagree
1. The people I supervise have trouble getting along with each other.	1	2	3	4	5
2. My subordinates are reliable and trustworthy.	5	4	3	2	1
3. There seems to be a friendly atmosphere among the people I supervise.	5	4	3	2	1
4. My subordinates always cooperate with me in getting the job done.	5	4	3	2	1
5. There is friction between my subordinates and myself.	1	2	3	4	5
6. My subordinates give me a good deal of help and support in getting the job done.	5	4	3	2	1
7. The people I supervise work well together in getting the job done.	5	4	3	2	1
8. I have good relations with the people I supervise.	5	4	3	2	1

Total Score [   ]

TASK STRUCTURE RATING SCALE—PART 1

Circle the number in the appropriate column.	Usually True	Sometimes True	Seldom True
Is the Goal Clearly Stated or Known?			
1. Is there a blueprint, picture, model or detailed description available of the finished product or service?	2	1	0
2. Is there a person available to advise and give a description of the finished product or service, or how the job should be done?	2	1	0
Is There Only One Way to Accomplish the Task?			
3. Is there a step-by-step procedure, or a standard operating procedure which indicates in detail the process which is to be followed?	2	1	0
4. Is there a specific way to subdivide the task into separate parts or steps?	2	1	0
5. Are there some ways which are clearly recognized as better than others for performing this task?	2	1	0
Is There Only One Correct Answer or Solution?			
6. Is it obvious when the task is finished and the correct solution has been found?	2	1	0
7. Is there a book, manual, or job description which indicates the best solution or the best outcome for the task?	2	1	0
Is It Easy to Check Whether the Job Was Done Right?			
8. Is there a generally agreed upon understanding about the standards the particular product or service has to meet to be considered acceptable?	2	1	0
9. Is the evaluation of this task generally made on some quantitative basis?	2	1	0
10. Can the leader and the group find out how well the task has been accomplished in enough time to improve future performance?	2	1	0

SUBTOTAL _____

TASK STRUCTURE RATING SCALE—PART 2

Training and Experience Adjustment

NOTE: Do not adjust jobs with task structure scores of 6 or below.

a. Compared to others in this or similar positions, how much *training* has the leader had?

3	2	1	0
No training at all	Very little training	A moderate amount of training	A great deal of training

b. Compared to others in this or similar positions, how much *experience* has the leader had?

6	4	2	0
No experience at all	Very little experience	A moderate amount of experience	A great deal of experience

Add lines (a) and (b) of the training and experience adjustment, then *subtract* this from the subtotal given in Part 1.

Subtotal from Part 1.

Subtract training and experience adjustment

Total Task Structure Score

POSITION POWER RATING SCALE

Circle the number which best represents your answer.

1. Can the leader directly or by recommendation administer rewards and punishments to subordinates?

2	1	0
Can act directly or can recommend with high effectiveness	Can recommend but with mixed results	No

2. Can the leader directly or by recommendation affect the promotion, demotion, hiring or firing of subordinates?

2	1	0
Can act directly or can recommend with high effectiveness	Can recommend but with mixed results	No

3. Does the leader have the knowledge necessary to assign tasks to subordinates and instruct them in task completion?

2	1	0
Yes	Sometimes or in some aspects	No

4. Is it the leader's job to evaluate the performance of subordinates?

2	1	0
Yes	Sometimes or in some aspects	No

5. Has the leader been given some official title of authority by the organization (e.g., foreman, department head, platoon leader)?

2	0
Yes	No

Total

SITUATIONAL CONTROL SCALE

Enter the total scores for the Leader-Member Relations dimension, the Task Structure scale, and the Position Power scale in the spaces below. Add the three scores together and compare your total with the ranges given in the table below to determine your overall situational control.

1. *Leader-Member Relations Total*

2. *Task Structure Total*

3. *Position Power Total*

Grand Total

Total Score	51 – 70	31 – 50	10 – 30
Amount of Situational Control	High Control	Moderate Control	Low Control

FEEDBACK

LEADER-MEMBER RELATIONS SCALE

Circle the number which best represents your response to each item.

	strongly agree	agree	neither agree nor disagree	disagree	strongly disagree
1. The people I supervise have trouble getting along with each other.	1	2	3	4	(5)
2. My subordinates are reliable and trustworthy.	(5)	4	3	2	1
3. There seems to be a friendly atmosphere among the people I supervise.	(5)	4	3	2	1
4. My subordinates always cooperate with me in getting the job done.	5	4	(3)	2	1
5. There is friction between my subordinates and myself.	1	2	(3)	4	5
6. My subordinates give me a good deal of help and support in getting the job done.	5	4	(3)	2	1
7. The people I supervise work well together in getting the job done.	(5)	4	3	2	1
8. I have good relations with the people I supervise.	5	4	(3)	2	1

Total Score   32

FEEDBACK

TASK STRUCTURE RATING SCALE—PART 1

Circle the number in the appropriate column.	Usually True	Sometimes True	Seldom True
Is the Goal Clearly Stated or Known?			
1. Is there a blueprint, picture, model or detailed description available of the finished product or service?	(2)	1	0
2. Is there a person available to advise and give a description of the finished product or service, or how the job should be done?	2	(1)	0
Is There Only One Way to Accomplish the Task?			
3. Is there a step-by-step procedure, or a standard operating procedure which indicates in detail the process which is to be followed?	(2)	1	0
4. Is there a specific way to subdivide the task into separate parts or steps?	(2)	1	0
5. Are there some ways which are clearly recognized as better than others for performing this task?	(2)	1	0
Is There Only One Correct Answer or Solution?			
6. Is it obvious when the task is finished and the correct solution has been found?	(2)	1	0
7. Is there a book, manual, or job description which indicates the best solution or the best outcome for the task?	2	(1)	0
Is It Easy to Check Whether the Job Was Done Right?			
8. Is there a generally agreed upon understanding about the standards the particular product or service has to meet to be considered acceptable?	(2)	1	0
9. Is the evaluation of this task generally made on some quantitative basis?	2	(1)	0
10. Can the leader and the group find out how well the task has been accomplished in enough time to improve future performance?	(2)	1	0

SUBTOTAL ____17____

125

FEEDBACK

TASK STRUCTURE RATING SCALE—PART 2

Training and Experience Adjustment

NOTE: Do not adjust jobs with task structure scores of 6 or below.

a. Compared to others in this or similar positions, how much *training* has the leader had?

3	2	1	(0)
No training at all	Very little training	A moderate amount of training	A great deal of training

b. Compared to others in this or similar positions, how much *experience* has the leader had?

6	4	(2)	0
No experience at all	Very little experience	A moderate amount of experience	A great deal of experience

Add lines (a) and (b) of the training and experience adjustment, then *subtract* this from the subtotal given in Part 1.

Subtotal from Part 1.

$$\boxed{17}$$

Subtract training and experience adjustment

$$\boxed{-2}$$

Total Task Structure Score

$$\boxed{15}$$

FEEDBACK

POSITION POWER RATING SCALE

Circle the number which best represents your answer.

1. Can the leader directly or by recommendation administer rewards and punishments to subordinates?

(2)	1	0
Can act directly or can recommend with high effectiveness	Can recommend but with mixed results	No

2. Can the leader directly or by recommendation affect the promotion, demotion, hiring or firing of subordinates?

(2)	1	0
Can act directly or can recommend with high effectiveness	Can recommend but with mixed results	No

3. Does the leader have the knowledge necessary to assign tasks to subordinates and instruct them in task completion?

(2)	1	0
Yes	Sometimes or in some aspects	No

4. Is it the leader's job to evaluate the performance of subordinates?

(2)	1	0
Yes	Sometimes or in some aspects	No

5. Has the leader been given some official title of authority by the organization (e.g., foreman, department head, platoon leader)?

(2)	0
Yes	No

Total   10

FEEDBACK

SITUATIONAL CONTROL SCALE

Enter the total scores for the Leader-Member Relations dimension, the Task Structure scale, and the Position Power scale in the spaces below. Add the three scores together and compare your total with the ranges given in the table below to determine your overall situational control.

1. *Leader-Member Relations Total*   32

2. *Task Structure Total*   15

3. *Position Power Total*   10

Grand Total   57

Total Score	51 – 70	31 – 50	10 – 30
Amount of Situational Control	High Control	Moderate Control	Low Control

FEEDBACK

As the short description indicated to you, morale and leader-member relations in the company are generally very good, and there is no reason to expect that the shipping supervisor will have any difficulties. A score of 32 would be appropriate on the LMR scale; however, a score of 30 or above would be acceptable. You will notice that we have scored questions 4,5,6, and 8 as neither agree nor disagree. This was done because we do not know for sure how the new shipping manager will get along with subordinates in the department. We have no reason to believe their relationship will be poor, but we do not know that it will be exceptionally good. The best strategy in this case is to select the middle answer, neither agree nor disagree. The rest of the questions, however, should receive the maximum points since we do know the group members get along well with each other.

Task structure is, of course, quite high for this job. Note that the shipping manager is not required to innovate in managing shipping docks, completing paperwork, and seeing that goods are properly routed. We rated all questions except 2, 7, and 9 on the task structure scales as "usually." Question 2 received a "sometimes" since the manager probably does not have someone available to seek advice from at all times. Question 7 was scored "sometimes" since the shipping dock job would not have a written manual providing all the best solutions or outcomes. Obviously, the manager will have to make some decisions on his or her own. Question 9 received a "sometimes" since there is little quantitative evaluation made of shipping procedures. This provided us with a subtotal of 17. Because the manager would receive an extensive training program, there was no training adjustment. However, because the manager's experience was "adequate" in a nonsupervisory job, we subtracted two points from the total score. The task structure score was 15. If your score was above 14, you understood the problem well.

The position power is that of a line manager and is quite high. You could safely have answered with the maximum points for all questions. However, if your score is above 7, you are in the right range.

This would give you a total situational control score of 57: a situation of high control. If your score was over 50, you did well and should move on to the next probe. If you missed this one, carefully compare your scales to the feedback to determine where you made your mistake.

PROBE 16

You are the assistant to the Director of Employee Relations for a large (8,000 employees) manufacturing company. The morale of the firm is quite good; profits are up and, by and large, the workers are satisfied. The company has decided to organize an extensive recreational program available to all employees and a committee is being set up to study the question.

You have been selected to chair the committee, and you can choose your own committee members. Therefore, interpersonal relations should be excellent. As chairperson, you will have no official power, but will simply coordinate and guide the work of the committee.

What is your estimate of situational control for this job?

High control _____
Moderate control _____
Low control _____

Rate the situational control for this job and compare these ratings with the estimate you have made. Then look at the feedback and see how close you came to the ratings we provided.

LEADER-MEMBER RELATIONS SCALE

Circle the number which best represents your response to each item.

	strongly agree	agree	neither agree nor disagree	disagree	strongly disagree
1. The people I supervise have trouble getting along with each other.	1	2	3	4	5
2. My subordinates are reliable and trustworthy.	5	4	3	2	1
3. There seems to be a friendly atmosphere among the people I supervise.	5	4	3	2	1
4. My subordinates always cooperate with me in getting the job done.	5	4	3	2	1
5. There is friction between my subordinates and myself.	1	2	3	4	5
6. My subordinates give me a good deal of help and support in getting the job done.	5	4	3	2	1
7. The people I supervise work well together in getting the job done.	5	4	3	2	1
8. I have good relations with the people I supervise.	5	4	3	2	1

Total Score

TASK STRUCTURE RATING SCALE—PART 1

Circle the number in the appropriate column.	Usually True	Sometimes True	Seldom True
Is the Goal Clearly Stated or Known?			
1. Is there a blueprint, picture, model or detailed description available of the finished product or service?	2	1	0
2. Is there a person available to advise and give a description of the finished product or service, or how the job should be done?	2	1	0
Is There Only One Way to Accomplish the Task?			
3. Is there a step-by-step procedure, or a standard operating procedure which indicates in detail the process which is to be followed?	2	1	0
4. Is there a specific way to subdivide the task into separate parts or steps?	2	1	0
5. Are there some ways which are clearly recognized as better than others for performing this task?	2	1	0
Is There Only One Correct Answer or Solution?			
6. Is it obvious when the task is finished and the correct solution has been found?	2	1	0
7. Is there a book, manual, or job description which indicates the best solution or the best outcome for the task?	2	1	0
Is It Easy to Check Whether the Job Was Done Right?			
8. Is there a generally agreed upon understanding about the standards the particular product or service has to meet to be considered acceptable?	2	1	0
9. Is the evaluation of this task generally made on some quantitative basis?	2	1	0
10. Can the leader and the group find out how well the task has been accomplished in enough time to improve future performance?	2	1	0
SUBTOTAL	_____		

TASK STRUCTURE RATING SCALE—PART 2

Training and Experience Adjustment

NOTE: Do not adjust jobs with task structure scores of 6 or below.

a. Compared to others in this or similar positions, how much *training* has the leader had?

3	2	1	0
No training at all	Very little training	A moderate amount of training	A great deal of training

b. Compared to others in this or similar positions, how much *experience* has the leader had?

6	4	2	0
No experience at all	Very little experience	A moderate amount of experience	A great deal of experience

Add lines (a) and (b) of the training and experience adjustment, then *subtract* this from the subtotal given in Part 1.

Subtotal from Part 1.

Subtract training and experience adjustment

Total Task Structure Score

POSITION POWER RATING SCALE

Circle the number which best represents your answer.

1. Can the leader directly or by recommendation administer rewards and punishments to subordinates?

2	1	0
Can act directly or can recommend with high effectiveness	Can recommend but with mixed results	No

2. Can the leader directly or by recommendation affect the promotion, demotion, hiring or firing of subordinates?

2	1	0
Can act directly or can recommend with high effectiveness	Can recommend but with mixed results	No

3. Does the leader have the knowledge necessary to assign tasks to subordinates and instruct them in task completion?

2	1	0
Yes	Sometimes or in some aspects	No

4. Is it the leader's job to evaluate the performance of subordinates?

2	1	0
Yes	Sometimes or in some aspects	No

5. Has the leader been given some official title of authority by the organization (e.g., foreman, department head, platoon leader)?

2	0
Yes	No

Total

SITUATIONAL CONTROL SCALE

Enter the total scores for the Leader-Member Relations dimension, the Task Structure scale, and the Position Power scale in the spaces below. Add the three scores together and compare your total with the ranges given in the table below to determine your overall situational control.

1. *Leader-Member Relations Total*

2. *Task Structure Total*

3. *Position Power Total*

Grand Total

Total Score	51 – 70	31 – 50	10 – 30
Amount of Situational Control	High Control	Moderate Control	Low Control

FEEDBACK

LEADER-MEMBER RELATIONS SCALE

Circle the number which best represents your response to each item.

	strongly agree	agree	neither agree nor disagree	disagree	strongly disagree
1. The people I supervise have trouble getting along with each other.	1	2	3	4	(5)
2. My subordinates are reliable and trustworthy.	(5)	4	3	2	1
3. There seems to be a friendly atmosphere among the people I supervise.	(5)	4	3	2	1
4. My subordinates always cooperate with me in getting the job done.	(5)	4	3	2	1
5. There is friction between my subordinates and myself.	1	2	3	4	(5)
6. My subordinates give me a good deal of help and support in getting the job done.	(5)	4	3	2	1
7. The people I supervise work well together in getting the job done.	(5)	4	3	2	1
8. I have good relations with the people I supervise.	(5)	4	3	2	1

Total Score   *40*

FEEDBACK

TASK STRUCTURE RATING SCALE—PART 1

Circle the number in the appropriate column.	Usually True	Sometimes True	Seldom True
Is the Goal Clearly Stated or Known?			
1. Is there a blueprint, picture, model or detailed description available of the finished product or service?	2	1	(0)
2. Is there a person available to advise and give a description of the finished product or service, or how the job should be done?	2	1	(0)
Is There Only One Way to Accomplish the Task?			
3. Is there a step-by-step procedure, or a standard operating procedure which indicates in detail the process which is to be followed?	2	1	(0)
4. Is there a specific way to subdivide the task into separate parts or steps?	2	1	(0)
5. Are there some ways which are clearly recognized as better than others for performing this task?	2	(1)	0
Is There Only One Correct Answer or Solution?			
6. Is it obvious when the task is finished and the correct solution has been found?	2	1	(0)
7. Is there a book, manual, or job description which indicates the best solution or the best outcome for the task?	2	1	(0)
Is It Easy to Check Whether the Job Was Done Right?			
8. Is there a generally agreed upon understanding about the standards the particular product or service has to meet to be considered acceptable?	2	1	0
9. Is the evaluation of this task generally made on some quantitative basis?	2	(1)	0
10. Can the leader and the group find out how well the task has been accomplished in enough time to improve future performance?	2	(1)	0

SUBTOTAL _____3_____

FEEBACK

TASK STRUCTURE RATING SCALE—PART 2

Training and Experience Adjustment

NOTE: Do not adjust jobs with task structure scores of 6 or below.

a. Compared to others in this or similar positions, how much *training* has the leader had?

3	2	1	0
No training at all	Very little training	A moderate amount of training	A great deal of training

b. Compared to others in this or similar positions, how much *experience* has the leader had?

6	4	2	0
No experience at all	Very little experience	A moderate amount of experience	A great deal of experience

Add lines (a) and (b) of the training and experience adjustment, then *subtract* this from the subtotal given in Part 1.

Subtotal from Part 1.   3

Subtract training and experience adjustment   − *

Total Task Structure Score   3

*No adjustment necessary since Part 1 score is less than 6.

FEEDBACK

POSITION POWER RATING SCALE

Circle the number which best represents your answer.

1. Can the leader directly or by recommendation administer rewards and punishments to subordinates?

2	1	(0)
Can act directly or can recommend with high effectiveness	Can recommend but with mixed results	No

2. Can the leader directly or by recommendation affect the promotion, demotion, hiring or firing of subordinates?

2	1	(0)
Can act directly or can recommend with high effectiveness	Can recommend but with mixed results	No

3. Does the leader have the knowledge necessary to assign tasks to subordinates and instruct them in task completion?

2	1	(0)
Yes	Sometimes or in some aspects	No

4. Is it the leader's job to evaluate the performance of subordinates?

2	1	(0)
Yes	Sometimes or in some aspects	No

5. Has the leader been given some official title of authority by the organization (e.g., foreman, department head, platoon leader)?

(2)	0
Yes	No

Total | 2 |

FEEDBACK

SITUATIONAL CONTROL SCALE

Enter the total scores for the Leader-Member Relations dimension, the Task Structure scale, and the Position Power scale in the spaces below. Add the three scores together and compare your total with the ranges given in the table below to determine your overall situational control.

1. *Leader-Member Relations Total* 40

2. *Task Structure Total* 3

3. *Position Power Total* 2

Grand Total 45

Total Score	51 – 70	31 – 50	10 – 30
Amount of Situational Control	High Control	Moderate Control	Low Control

FEEDBACK

You are, of course, told that leader-member relations are quite good. But even if you had not been given this information, chances are that the job of chairing a committee to organize a recreational program will probably not create too much tension. A score of 25–40 would be appropriate.

The TASK here would be HIGHLY UNSTRUCTURED. To be sure, the committee is to propose a recreational program, but the nature of the program, its organization, and details of its implementation are all left open. On the task structure rating scale all items except 5, 9, and 10 received "seldom," thereby accumulating scores of zero.

Questions 9 and 10 also scored 1 point each since there would be some opportunity, as you progress on the project, to get feedback on whether the recreational program is adequate. Because the total score is so low, no training and experience adjustment is required. A score of 3 is about right.

Committee chairs usually will have very low position power. About the only place this job would score high on the position power scale would be question 5—the chairperson does have an official title. This would be worth 2 points.

Basically, the relations between the chairperson and members will be good and the task will be unstructured, having low position power. This situation, therefore, would be moderate in control. A score of 45 would be appropriate.

If you got this one right, you are on the way to being an expert. Keep up the good work.

PROBE 17

You have been selected as the director of a laboratory for research and development of a large plastics firm. Your predecessor was fired for maintaining sloppy financial records and accounting procedures, and for poor management of the laboratory's program.

The rest of the laboratory research staff is quite upset and several have considered quitting. Much hostility exists between the research staff and management. Although complete information on the situation is not available, the leader-member relations with the acting director are quite strained. In fact, this interim director filled out a leader-member relations scale for you and came up with a score of 16.

You have been working in another laboratory on the West Coast and feel you have average experience and training for the job. As before, you will supervise the research staff and be responsible for evaluating the staff and recommending changes. These recommendations will be given consideration by upper management along with other available information.

As in practically all research efforts, there is no way to specify exactly how the work is to be done and what procedures are to be followed in seeking new products or in developing new programs. The expectation is, however, that the laboratory will come up with marketable products that will benefit the company.

What is your estimate of the situational control for this job?

High control _____
Moderate control _____
Low control _____

On the following pages rate the situational control for the job and compare these ratings with the estimate you have made. Then look at the feedback, and see how close you came to the ratings we provided.

LEADER-MEMBER RELATIONS SCALE

Circle the number which best represents your response to each item.

	strongly agree	agree	neither agree nor disagree	disagree	strongly disagree
1. The people I supervise have trouble getting along with each other.	1	2	③	4	5
2. My subordinates are reliable and trustworthy.	5	4	3	②	1
3. There seems to be a friendly atmosphere among the people I supervise.	5	4	3	②	1
4. My subordinates always cooperate with me in getting the job done.	5	4	③	2	1
5. There is friction between my subordinates and myself.	①	2	3	4	5
6. My subordinates give me a good deal of help and support in getting the job done.	5	4	3	②	1
7. The people I supervise work well together in getting the job done.	5	4	3	2	①
8. I have good relations with the people I supervise.	5	4	3	②	1

Total Score | 16 |*

*according to the interim director's LMR rating

TASK STRUCTURE RATING SCALE—PART 1

Circle the number in the appropriate column.	Usually True	Sometimes True	Seldom True
Is the Goal Clearly Stated or Known?			
1. Is there a blueprint, picture, model or detailed description available of the finished product or service?	2	1	0
2. Is there a person available to advise and give a description of the finished product or service, or how the job should be done?	2	1	0
Is There Only One Way to Accomplish the Task?			
3. Is there a step-by-step procedure, or a standard operating procedure which indicates in detail the process which is to be followed?	2	1	0
4. Is there a specific way to subdivide the task into separate parts or steps?	2	1	0
5. Are there some ways which are clearly recognized as better than others for performing this task?	2	1	0
Is There Only One Correct Answer or Solution?			
6. Is it obvious when the task is finished and the correct solution has been found?	2	1	0
7. Is there a book, manual, or job description which indicates the best solution or the best outcome for the task?	2	1	0
Is It Easy to Check Whether the Job Was Done Right?			
8. Is there a generally agreed upon understanding about the standards the particular product or service has to meet to be considered acceptable?	2	1	0
9. Is the evaluation of this task generally made on some quantitative basis?	2	1	0
10. Can the leader and the group find out how well the task has been accomplished in enough time to improve future performance?	2	1	0

SUBTOTAL _____

TASK STRUCTURE RATING SCALE—PART 2

Training and Experience Adjustment

NOTE: Do not adjust jobs with task structure scores of 6 or below.

a. Compared to others in this or similar positions, how much *training* has the leader had?

3	2	1	0
No training at all	Very little training	A moderate amount of training	A great deal of training

b. Compared to others in this or similar positions, how much *experience* has the leader had?

6	4	2	0
No experience at all	Very little experience	A moderate amount of experience	A great deal of experience

Add lines (a) and (b) of the training and experience adjustment, then *subtract* this from the subtotal given in Part 1.

Subtotal from Part 1.

Subtract training and experience adjustment

Total Task Structure Score

POSITION POWER RATING SCALE

Circle the number which best represents your answer.

1. Can the leader directly or by recommendation administer rewards and punishments to subordinates?

2	1	0
Can act directly or can recommend with high effectiveness	Can recommend but with mixed results	No

2. Can the leader directly or by recommendation affect the promotion, demotion, hiring or firing of subordinates?

2	1	0
Can act directly or can recommend with high effectiveness	Can recommend but with mixed results	No

3. Does the leader have the knowledge necessary to assign tasks to subordinates and instruct them in task completion?

2	1	0
Yes	Sometimes or in some aspects	No

4. Is it the leader's job to evaluate the performance of subordinates?

2	1	0
Yes	Sometimes or in some aspects	No

5. Has the leader been given some official title of authority by the organization (e.g., foreman, department head, platoon leader)?

2	0
Yes	No

Total

SITUATIONAL CONTROL SCALE

Enter the total scores for the Leader-Member Relations dimension, the Task Structure scale, and the Position Power scale in the spaces below. Add the three scores together and compare your total with the ranges given in the table below to determine your overall situational control.

1. *Leader-Member Relations Total*

2. *Task Structure Total*

3. *Position Power Total*

Grand Total

Total Score	51 – 70	31 – 50	10 – 30
Amount of Situational Control	High Control	Moderate Control	Low Control

FEEDBACK

LEADER-MEMBER RELATIONS SCALE

Circle the number which best represents your response to each item.

	strongly agree	agree	neither agree nor disagree	disagree	strongly disagree
1. The people I supervise have trouble getting along with each other.	1	2	(3)	4	5
2. My subordinates are reliable and trustworthy.	5	4	3	(2)	1
3. There seems to be a friendly atmosphere among the people I supervise.	5	4	3	(2)	1
4. My subordinates always cooperate with me in getting the job done.	5	4	(3)	2	1
5. There is friction between my subordinates and myself.	(1)	2	3	4	5
6. My subordinates give me a good deal of help and support in getting the job done.	5	4	3	(2)	1
7. The people I supervise work well together in getting the job done.	5	4	3	2	(1)
8. I have good relations with the people I supervise.	5	4	3	(2)	1

Total Score | *16* *

according to the interim director's LMR rating

FEEDBACK

TASK STRUCTURE RATING SCALE—PART 1

Circle the number in the appropriate column.	Usually True	Sometimes True	Seldom True
Is the Goal Clearly Stated or Known?			
1. Is there a blueprint, picture, model or detailed description available of the finished product or service?	2	1	(0)
2. Is there a person available to advise and give a description of the finished product or service, or how the job should be done?	2	(1)	0
Is There Only One Way to Accomplish the Task?			
3. Is there a step-by-step procedure, or a standard operating procedure which indicates in detail the process which is to be followed?	2	1	(0)
4. Is there a specific way to subdivide the task into separate parts or steps?	2	(1)	0
5. Are there some ways which are clearly recognized as better than others for performing this task?	2	(1)	0
Is There Only One Correct Answer or Solution?			
6. Is it obvious when the task is finished and the correct solution has been found?	2	(1)	0
7. Is there a book, manual, or job description which indicates the best solution or the best outcome for the task?	2	1	(0)
Is It Easy to Check Whether the Job Was Done Right?			
8. Is there a generally agreed upon understanding about the standards the particular product or service has to meet to be considered acceptable?	2	(1)	0
9. Is the evaluation of this task generally made on some quantitative basis?	2	1	(0)
10. Can the leader and the group find out how well the task has been accomplished in enough time to improve future performance?	2	1	(0)
SUBTOTAL	*5*		

FEEDBACK

TASK STRUCTURE RATING SCALE—PART 2

Training and Experience Adjustment

NOTE: Do not adjust jobs with task structure scores of 6 or below.

a. Compared to others in this or similar positions, how much *training* has the leader had?

3	2	1	0
No training at all	Very little training	A moderate amount of training	A great deal of training

b. Compared to others in this or similar positions, how much *experience* has the leader had?

6	4	2	0
No experience at all	Very little experience	A moderate amount of experience	A great deal of experience

Add lines (a) and (b) of the training and experience adjustment, then *subtract* this from the subtotal given in Part 1.

Subtotal from Part 1.

    5

Subtract training and experience adjustment

    -

Total Task Structure Score

    5

FEEDBACK

POSITION POWER RATING SCALE

Circle the number which best represents your answer.

1. Can the leader directly or by recommendation administer rewards and punishments to subordinates?

2	(1)	0
Can act directly or can recommend with high effectiveness	Can recommend but with mixed results	No

2. Can the leader directly or by recommendation affect the promotion, demotion, hiring or firing of subordinates?

2	(1)	0
Can act directly or can recommend with high effectiveness	Can recommend but with mixed results	No

3. Does the leader have the knowledge necessary to assign tasks to subordinates and instruct them in task completion?

2	(1)	0
Yes	Sometimes or in some aspects	No

4. Is it the leader's job to evaluate the performance of subordinates?

(2)	1	0
Yes	Sometimes or in some aspects	No

5. Has the leader been given some official title of authority by the organization (e.g., foreman, department head, platoon leader)?

(2)	0
Yes	No

Total 7

FEEDBACK

SITUATIONAL CONTROL SCALE

Enter the total scores for the Leader-Member Relations dimension, the Task Structure scale, and the Position Power scale in the spaces below. Add the three scores together and compare your total with the ranges given in the table below to determine your overall situational control.

1. *Leader-Member Relations Total*

$\boxed{16}$

2. *Task Structure Total*

$\boxed{5}$

3. *Position Power Total*

$\boxed{7}$

Grand Total $\boxed{28}$

Total Score	51 – 70	31 – 50	10 – 30
Amount of Situational Control	High Control	Moderate Control	Low Control

FEEDBACK

If you rated this position as falling into the low control zone (scale value of 28), you were, of course, correct in your assessment. The fact that the research staff was upset and at the point of quitting is compelling information and closely agrees with the LMR rating of 16.

The task structure is clearly low in this case. A research director's job cannot be considered high in structure, especially when the goal is the development of new products rather than making minor improvement in old ones.

The position power also should have given you no trouble. A director who can hire and fire has clout. This is, however, mitigated by the fact that the leader in this situation must depend on a staff of experts and that this dependence on their good judgment and willingness to do a good job reduces the power available.

How did you do on these three probes? If you had trouble, review the chapters that gave you the most difficulty. Be sure you understand how to determine situational control before continuing with the program.

If you got all three probes right, you are ready to continue. Review the concepts you have learned in the Part II summary that follows, and then check your understanding of the program by completing the Part II Self-Test.

SUMMARY OF PART II

Part II introduced you to methods for measuring the amount of control and influence you have over your leadership situation and the outcomes of your decisions. The amount of control you have is determined by evaluating your job on three dimensions:

Leader-Member Relations: How well the group and the leader get along. This is the most important dimension.

Task Structure: The degree to which the job is clearly defined. This is second in importance to leader-member relations and worth half the value in determining situational control.

Position Power: The leader's conferred authority to hire, fire, and discipline which is third in importance in determining situational control.

The combination of these three factors determines situational control, which is divided into three ranges of high, moderate, and low.

High Control: The leader has a great deal of control and influence, exemplified by good leader-member relations, a structured task, and high position power.

Moderate Control: Situations in which the leader typically is presented with a mixed picture—either good relations with subordinates but an unstructured task and low position power; or the reverse, poor relations, but a structured task and high position power.

Low Control   Situations in which the leader's control and influence are relatively low. That is, the group does not support the leader, and neither the task nor position power give the leader much influence. This is more challenging, and tends to be a more stressful situation.

You are now ready for Part III, which shows you how to match situations to the leader's personality. Included in this part is a chapter on how to engineer your own leadership situation to fit your leadership style.

Before going on, take the Part II Self-Test.

PART II SELF-TEST

1. The second most important factor in determining situational control is _____.

2. A situation in which the leader has good relations with his subordinates and an unstructured task with low position power would be one of high/moderate/low _____ situational control.

3. The scale used to measure your relations with your group is called _____.

4. A situation in which the leader has poor leader-member relations, low position power, and an unstructured task would be one of high/moderate/low _____ situational control.

5. The amount of authority you have in a given situation can be measured by the _____ scale.

6. The three dimensions used to determine the situational control in order of their importance are as follows (check the correct choice):

   ____a. 1. Task Structure
           2. Position Power
           3. Leader-Member Relations
   ____b. 1. Leader-Member Relations
           2. Position Power
           3. Task Structure
   ____c. 1. Leader-Member Relations
           2. Task Structure
           3. Position Power

7. A situation in which the leader has good leader-member relations, high position power, and a structured task would be one of high/moderate/low _____ situational control.

Answers to Part II Self-Test

The correct answers to the Part II Self-Test are:

1. task structure

2. moderate situational control

3. LMR scale

4. low situational control

5. position power scale

6. (c)

7. high situational control

If you missed any of these items, be sure to review the relevant material before you go on.

COMPUTING SITUATIONAL CONTROL FOR YOUR PRIMARY LEADERSHIP JOB

Now that you have had considerable practice with all of the scales that measure the various aspects of leadership control and have determined your leadership style, you are ready to analyze your own leadership situation.

On the following pages are scales you should complete to determine the amount of control you have in your primary leadership situation—either your present leadership job or your most important past leadership role. Score each scale, and then compute the overall rating. Locate your score on the table to determine the amount of situational control for this job.

The next chapter will discuss what to do if you find that your primary leadership job does not match your leadership style. Conversely, if you are in the right situation, you will see how to maintain this successful match.

LEADER-MEMBER RELATIONS SCALE

Circle the number which best represents your response to each item.

	strongly agree	agree	neither agree nor disagree	disagree	strongly disagree
1. The people I supervise have trouble getting along with each other.	1	2	3	4	5
2. My subordinates are reliable and trustworthy.	5	4	3	2	1
3. There seems to be a friendly atmosphere among the people I supervise.	5	4	3	2	1
4. My subordinates always cooperate with me in getting the job done.	5	4	3	2	1
5. There is friction between my subordinates and myself.	1	2	3	4	5
6. My subordinates give me a good deal of help and support in getting the job done.	5	4	3	2	1
7. The people I supervise work well together in getting the job done.	5	4	3	2	1
8. I have good relations with the people I supervise.	5	4	3	2	1

Total Score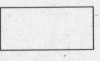

TASK STRUCTURE RATING SCALE—PART 1

Circle the number in the appropriate column.	Usually True	Sometimes True	Seldom True
Is the Goal Clearly Stated or Known?			
1. Is there a blueprint, picture, model or detailed description available of the finished product or service?	2	1	0
2. Is there a person available to advise and give a description of the finished product or service, or how the job should be done?	2	1	0
Is There Only One Way to Accomplish the Task?			
3. Is there a step-by-step procedure, or a standard operating procedure which indicates in detail the process which is to be followed?	2	1	0
4. Is there a specific way to subdivide the task into separate parts or steps?	2	1	0
5. Are there some ways which are clearly recognized as better than others for performing this task?	2	1	0
Is There Only One Correct Answer or Solution?			
6. Is it obvious when the task is finished and the correct solution has been found?	2	1	0
7. Is there a book, manual, or job description which indicates the best solution or the best outcome for the task?	2	1	0
Is It Easy to Check Whether the Job Was Done Right?			
8. Is there a generally agreed upon understanding about the standards the particular product or service has to meet to be considered acceptable?	2	1	0
9. Is the evaluation of this task generally made on some quantitative basis?	2	1	0
10. Can the leader and the group find out how well the task has been accomplished in enough time to improve future performance?	2	1	0

SUBTOTAL _____

TASK STRUCTURE RATING SCALE—PART 2

Training and Experience Adjustment

NOTE: Do not adjust jobs with task structure scores of 6 or below.

a. Compared to others in this or similar positions, how much *training* has the leader had?

3	2	1	0
No training at all	Very little training	A moderate amount of training	A great deal of training

b. Compared to others in this or similar positions, how much *experience* has the leader had?

6	4	2	0
No experience at all	Very little experience	A moderate amount of experience	A great deal of experience

Add lines (a) and (b) of the training and experience adjustment, then *subtract* this from the subtotal given in Part 1.

Subtotal from Part 1.

Subtract training and experience adjustment

Total Task Structure Score

POSITION POWER RATING SCALE

Circle the number which best represents your answer.

1. Can the leader directly or by recommendation administer rewards and punishments to subordinates?

2	1	0
Can act directly or can recommend with high effectiveness	Can recommend but with mixed results	No

2. Can the leader directly or by recommendation affect the promotion, demotion, hiring or firing of subordinates?

2	1	0
Can act directly or can recommend with high effectiveness	Can recommend but with mixed results	No

3. Does the leader have the knowledge necessary to assign tasks to subordinates and instruct them in task completion?

2	1	0
Yes	Sometimes or in some aspects	No

4. Is it the leader's job to evaluate the performance of subordinates?

2	1	0
Yes	Sometimes or in some aspects	No

5. Has the leader been given some official title of authority by the organization (e.g., foreman, department head, platoon leader)?

2	0
Yes	No

Total [ ]

SITUATIONAL CONTROL SCALE

Enter the total scores for the Leader-Member Relations dimension, the Task Structure scale, and the Position Power scale in the spaces below. Add the three scores together and compare your total with the ranges given in the table below to determine your overall situational control.

1. *Leader-Member Relations Total*

2. *Task Structure Total*

3. *Position Power Total*

Grand Total

Total Score	51 – 70	31 – 50	10 – 30
Amount of Situational Control	High Control	Moderate Control	Low Control

CREATING THE OPTIMAL LEADERSHIP ENVIRONMENT

8

**MATCHING YOUR
LEADERSHIP STYLE
WITH YOUR SITUATION**

The previous chapters told you how you can determine the degree of control you have in various leadership situations. If you are fortunate, the leadership situation will be just right for you. More often, it will not fit your leadership style exactly. Effective leadership requires that you match the situation to your particular leadership style.

In this chapter we will discuss the type of leadership situation that goes best with each type of leadership style. The next chapters will teach you how to modify your leadership situation to fit your leadership style and how you can apply your training to the management of leaders who work under your direction.

As we have said before, very few leaders are fortunate enough to function equally well in all situations under all conditions. Now that you know your own leadership style, you are ready to identify the kinds of situations in which you perform best.

The appropriate match between leadership style and situational control is shown below:

1. Task-motivated (low LPC) leaders perform best in situations of high control or low control.
2. Relationship-motivated (high LPC) leaders perform best in situations of moderate control. This is shown in Figure 8–1. The level of situational control is shown on the horizontal axis, performance is shown on the vertical axis. As you can see, each type of leadership works well in some conditions but not in others.

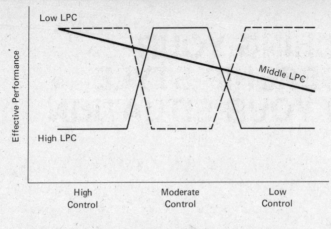

Figure 8–1   Schematic representation of the Contingency Model. Leadership performance is shown on the vertical axis, situational control on the horizontal axis. The solid, broken, and darker lines indicate the expected performance of high, low, and middle-LPC leaders respectively under the three situational control conditions.

Before we go on, let us briefly review once more the three categories of situational control:

____ 1. HIGH CONTROL: These are situations in which leaders have a predictable environment; that is, situations in which they have the support of the group members as well as a task which is highly structured so that everyone knows exactly what to do and how to do it. In addition, the leaders have relatively high position power, which enables them to back up their authority with appropriate rewards and punishment. In other words, leaders have a great deal of control and influence and can feel reasonably secure and certain that (a) their directions will be followed, and (b) their decisions will have the intended outcomes. This situation is best for the low LPC leader, and also seems to be best for the middle LPC leader.

____ 2. MODERATE CONTROL: These situations generally present mixed problems. Leaders may be supported by their group, but the task is relatively ambiguous and unstructured, and formal authority weak. Alternatively, the task might be structured and clear-cut, and the position power high, but the group members are nonsupportive. The leader, therefore, has to be diplomatic and tactful, and concerned with the feelings of group members in order to get their cooperation. This situation is best for the high LPC leader, but the middle LPC leader will also tend to perform well in this situation.

____ 3. LOW CONTROL: These situations are relatively difficult, more challenging, and sometimes quite stressful. The task is likely to be unstructured and unclear, and there MAY be no definite procedures or methods. Most importantly, leaders will feel that their group members do not like or support them and that they have little or no formal power to help them get things done. Even when they do have formal power and a structured task, a situation in which stress and anxiety are very high gives them VERY little control and assurance that they can determine the outcome. Some people prefer this kind of situation because they enjoy the challenge. This situation is best for the low LPC leader.

The table below summarizes the match between situations and different leadership styles.

If your leadership style and the situational control are properly matched, your performance as well as the group's output should be good. However, if your situational control does not match your leadership style, you may perform poorly and become dissatisfied or discouraged with your job. If you are mismatched, the next chapter will help you to determine how to change your situation. If you are in the right situation for your leadership style, the next chapter will tell you how to keep it that way.

Be sure to remember that the various scales for scoring and classifying situational control are guidelines, not ironclad rules. You must use your own judgment because there may well be some situations in which leader-member relations are so poor that the situation is low in control even though task structure and position power are high. There may also be situations in which position power is so strong that the other factors matter very little (e.g., a General supervising a team of enlisted men), or task structure so high that leader-member relations and position power do not mean much (e.g., the person in charge of a countdown of a space probe).

TABLE 8–1 Summary of Leadership Style, Behavior, and Performance in Varying Situations

Leader Type	High Control	Situational Control Moderate Control	Low Control
High LPC	*Behavior:* Somewhat autocratic, aloof and self-centered. Seemingly concerned with task. *Performance:* Poor	*Behavior:* Considerate, open, and participative. *Performance:* Good	*Behavior:* Anxious, tentative, overly concerned with interpersonal relations. *Performance:* Poor
Low LPC	*Behavior:* Considerate, and supportive. *Performance:* Good.	*Behavior:* Tense, task-focused. *Performance:* Poor.	*Behavior:* Directive, task-focused, serious. *Performance:* Relatively good.

By this time you should have enough experience estimating the three dimensions that you can apply the theory without using the specific scales. In the remainder of the program, you will base your decisions on your understanding of the Leader Match program rather than on scale scores.

If you have difficulty with a particular probe or would feel more confident in applying the theory, use the extra scales provided in the appendix. However, you should be able to diagnose situational control quickly and accurately so that you don't have to spend a lot of time filling out scales. The following probes illustrate the matching concept.

Turn to page 170 for Probe 18.

PROBE 18

You are the personnel director of a large company. A job has opened up for a middle-level manager in the accounting department and involves the supervision of several sections. All sections perform relatively routine bookkeeping, billing, and record keeping tasks. You consider this task highly structured and this evaluation is confirmed by several managers who completed the task structure scale.

You have every reason to believe that morale and employee satisfaction are high and that the department has generally had good relations between supervisors and employees. Moreover, the supervisors who would be reporting to the new manager are cooperative and eager to get along with management. Since the manager will have considerable authority, the position power is clearly high. Thus, situational control of the leadership position should be quite high. Most managers in the position stayed there for five or six years.

You have the job files on a number of junior executives who are eligible for this job and you are asked to make a recommendation.

Randolph Wallingford has been with the company for about five years. During the early years of his managerial career he held several unstructured staff jobs, which he performed passably well. He was then assigned to a management position of an accounting section in a branch office where he stayed for about one year. His performance again was passable but not distinguished.

He was then reassigned to manage an accounts receivable section, a structured and fairly routine job, where he has been for almost three years. He had a slow start but has become quite effective in the last year.

His subordinates feel that he is hard to get to know, although they like to work for him, and as long as they do their job he is easy to get along with. The LPC scale he completed on joining the firm indicates that he is task-motivated.

Joan Redmond is something of a company success story. Her first job was as assistant manager of the data processing department where she suggested a number of new procedures that have since been adopted. She requested a transfer after one year to a new billing department and again performed quite well. She seemed to run down after about two years and requested a transfer to sales. She seems to be seeking new and interesting jobs to broaden her experience.

Her fellow workers consider Joan easy to get along with, approachable, pleasant, and eager to make a good impression. Routine jobs tend to turn her off. Her LPC scale verifies that she is relationship-motivated.

John Leshi has held only one job in the company. When he first took the job, which involved keeping track of shipping and purchasing schedules, his performance was somewhat below the company's expectations, although his relations with coworkers were fairly good and he never had any major problems. He has remained in the same job without much improvement, and has not asked for a transfer or promotion. His job calls for no particular ingenuity, and he has shown no interest to make more of it. His leadership style is relationship-motivated according to his LPC score.

Considering that this is a high control situation, you decide to select:

_____ (a) Wallingford
_____ (b) Redmond
_____ (c) Leshi

Go to the next page for feedback.

FEEDBACK

a. **You chose (a):** *Randolph Wallingford.*

This is a good selection. His history of low performance in new and unstructured situations, or when first assigned to a management position confirms that he is task-motivated. This is further supported by the report that he is detached, hard to get to know, although easy to get along with as long as everyone does the job.

The leadership situation in the accounting department obviously provides high position power and high task structure. This is an ideal position for a task-motivated manager. Since most managers have stayed in this position for five or six years it would certainly be worthwhile to choose Wallingford, who is likely to become increasingly better as time goes on.

Notice here that LPC scales were available in company files and that you were able to verify the leadership style from descriptions of his behavior. As we've said before, you should try whenever possible to obtain LPC scores because that is the most accurate way to determine leadership style.

Good work! Now try Probe 19 on the next page.

b. **You chose (b):** *Joan Redmond.*

This is probably not the best choice. You can check that Redmond is relationship-motivated because, in the new situations she seeks out, she is easy to work with, approachable, pleasant, and eager to make a good impression. However, relationship-motivated people do not perform well in high control situations, and her history of asking for frequent transfers would indicate that she would not want to remain in the job as long as 5 or 6 years.

Go back to page 171 and make another choice.

c. **You chose (c):** *John Leshi.*

This is not such a good choice. From all indications, Leshi has held a structured job with high position power for several years and failed to improve. He seems a pleasant enough person but this is not one of the prime requisites of the job. His motivation seems questionable, so there is no reason to expect that Leshi will somehow blossom forth in a more difficult and demanding job, which this promotion would entail.

Go back to page 171 and make another choice.

PROBE 19

You are Director of a large manufacturing firm. The manager in charge of the advertising department just had a serious accident and has to be replaced since it is doubtful that he will be able to return to work for quite some time. You need someone to fill in for him.

The situation is rather hard to define. The key people are temperamental and touchy, and there has been a great deal of infighting and conflict. The manager has had a difficult time holding the department together. Moreover, there has been a demand from other managers for more creative marketing campaigns. You need someone who can immediately take charge of this department and make it productive.

Which kind of leader will you choose?

_____ (a) You pick a task-motivated (low LPC) leader.

_____ (b) You try to find a relationship-motivated (high LPC) person.

FEEDBACK

a. **You chose (a):** *You pick a task-motivated (low LPC) leader.*

This is the correct choice. Low LPC persons tend to perform best in situations in which their control and influence are either high or low, which is the case here. You noted that there is a great deal of tension and conflict among key people in the department, which suggests that the support these employees will give their manager will be unreliable at best, and probably quite poor. The task structure of an advertising department is very low, especially since there is a demand for more creative marketing, which places additional stress on this unstructured task.

Finally, the fact that the manager has been trying to hold the department together implies that he has been in danger of losing some of his important subordinates. The group's loyalty is, therefore, likely to be low. While the manager might have some formal position power, it would be very difficult to rely on disciplinary measures to keep the group in line. This is, therefore, clearly a low control situation.

You're doing well; now try Probe 20 on the next page.

b. **You chose (b):** *You try to find a relationship-motivated (high LPC) person.*

This is not the best answer. The manager of the advertising department has a very unstructured task, and he or she is under considerable pressure to come up with some creative new solutions to marketing problems. Under ordinary conditions, given good relations with subordinates and the typical power of a manager, this would call for a relationship-motivated leader. In this case, however, the situation provides the manager with very poor control. Not only is the task unstructured, but the key people in the group are engaged in infighting and are not likely to give wholehearted support to their manager. No matter which side the manager takes, somebody in the group will attack him or her for it. Moreover, the statement that the manager has been trying to keep the department together suggests that the manager is in a very weak position since subordinates must be placated and/or appeased. Even if the department manager had formal power to reward and punish, he or she probably could not really use it under these conditions. A relationship-motivated leader would not be able to work too well in this situation. Try again.

Now try Probe 20.

PROBE 20

You are a Vice-President of an electronics firm with plants in eight cities across the country. Recently several incidents suggesting a breach of security procedures have occurred in the patent products division on the West Coast. You must select a member of your staff and two others to go to the West Coast plant to investigate the problem.

Here are some of the facts that should be considered:

1. The local plant director and security officials will be unhappy to have an outside investigation. One aspect of the case is the possibility that the problem occurred because they paid inadequate attention to their duties.

2. This is a large facility with a heavy production schedule, so the investigation will have to be quite broad. Some standard investigative procedures will, of course, be followed but many decisions will have to be made as the investigation proceeds.

3. The head of the investigative team you send out will be given a special title and will have the major responsibility of recommending any procedural and/or personnel changes.

To decide which member of your staff is to head the team, you must first consider the situational control of the investigation. Based on your best off-the-cuff judgment, what is the situational control of this assignment?

_____ Low Control
_____ Moderate Control
_____ High Control

Given this situation, which of the following staff members would you choose as having the best chance of successfully accomplishing this assignment?

_____ Margaret Anderson—High LPC (Relationship-motivated)
_____ Randy Brannigan—Low LPC (Task-motivated)

Feedback is given on the following page.

FEEDBACK

The situation suggests, first of all, that the task structure is relatively low. The team will have to make decisions as the investigation progresses. Since the head of the team will be quite dependent upon his or her fellow team members, the position power also is likely to be low. However, a team of three people, forced to work in a relatively hostile environment (who likes an investigation?) is likely to stick together, and the leader-member relations are, therefore, apt to be quite good. This suggests that the assignment would have moderate situational control.

Margaret Anderson would, therefore, be your best choice, especially since high LPC people are able to manage somewhat better in difficult interpersonal situations, and investigating a problem of this nature is likely to be just that.

SUMMARY

The basic problem in leadership performance is the appropriate match between the leader's style or motivational pattern and the degree to which the leadership situation provides the leader with control and influence. As we said before, task-motivated leaders tend to perform best in high and low control situations, relationship-motivated leaders perform best in moderate control situations.

The problem for leaders consists of getting into, and remaining in, situations in which they can perform well. Knowing your leadership style and being able to identify the amount of control of the situation enables you to do this. Equally important, it should also make you aware of situations in which you are less likely to perform well. Remember,

If you learn to avoid situations in which you are likely to fail, you're bound to be a success.

The next chapter will discuss what to do if your leadership style and situational control do not make an appropriate match.

9

ENGINEERING YOUR OWN LEADERSHIP SITUATION

You will frequently end up in situations that do not match your particular leadership style. When this occurs you have two choices: You can change your leadership style—and your personality, which determines your style—or you can modify your leadership situation.

Let us remember, first of all, that your basic leadership style is part of your personality. It is the consistent way you behave in dealings with subordinates and superiors. This behavior is probably learned in early childhood and adolescence. The way you talk and interact with others in a work situation is as much a part of your personality as the way you behave toward your parents, friends, spouse, or children.

It is difficult to change less important behaviors: Consider the trouble people have when they try to stop smoking, or cure themselves of such habits as saying, "You know" after every couple of sentences.

It is even more difficult to change your basic leadership style. Practically speaking, it would be as difficult as suddenly trying to become a completely different person. If it were possible, everyone would be popular, lovable, and effective.

This is not to say that personality does not change, but such changes that do occur tend to be gradual and usually take many years. Your personality, and therefore your leadership style, will not change simply because you feel like changing it, or because somebody tells you to change it.

It is much easier to change your leadership situation than your personality. Although you may find this hard to believe at first, your ability to control your immediate leadership environment is considerably greater than most people may realize. This is true even of jobs that seem highly circumscribed and specific. Job engineering provides an important method for improving your own leadership performance and the effectiveness of your organization. How you do this is described in this chapter. And although you may be able to change your behavior to some extent, making such changes during a period of time when you are under pressure to improve immediate performance is not the best strategy.

How much you can modify or "engineer" your own leadership job depends on a number of factors. If your relationship with your boss allows you to talk freely with him (or her), and if he or she is supportive, it will be very easy to change a number of important dimensions of your leadership job. If your relationship with your boss does not allow you to discuss these issues, you will still be able to make some important changes. Remember, for instance, that the way you relate to your subordinates is under your own control and under no one else's. You must also remember that your good performance reflects well on your boss, and that it is to your boss's advantage to have a smoothly running department or work unit.

If the relationship with your boss is strained, your ability to make changes in your leadership situation will, of course, be more limited. But again, you are not helpless. It is part of your job, first of all, to "train" your boss, to let him or her know under what conditions you work best, and how he or she can make you most effective.

The method for doing so, again, is not too difficult: You must remember that bosses, no less than subordinates, respond to praise and signs of approval. How often has one of your subordinates told you that you are a good person to work for? And were you not pleased when it did occur? The basic principle is that you must give your boss a positive sign when he or she does something you want to happen more often. We shall return to this principle and the specific methods for doing so later on.

If possible, you should sit down with your boss to discuss the kinds of situations which seem to be most suitable for you, and the various ways in which you both could restructure your leadership situation so that it matches your particular leadership style. If your relationship with your boss does not permit you to do this, you will have to try to make some of the changes on your own.

Not surprisingly, the three components of the job situation—leader-member relations, task structure, and position power—are the areas in which you can most effectively modify your leadership situation. The three areas are dealt with below along with checklists of options which you may use to engineer your job situation.

MODIFYING LEADER-MEMBER RELATIONS

Some people naturally and easily establish a climate of good will and trust with their subordinates and develop close and lasting friendships with them. For others this is more difficult. If you wish to improve your leader-member relations, make sure that you clearly understand your subordinates' problems and that you try to alleviate them so that they get to know you as a person.

- You can try to provide them with accurate information about the organization so that you earn their trust and confidence.
- You might institute special "gripe sessions" or regular meetings to give your subordinates an opportunity to know you better.
- You might institute informal brown-bag lunches or occasionally go out after work with them to celebrate the successful completion of a particular task. You should be aware, however, that attempts to improve relations with subordinates must be honest. Insincerity or vacillation will be recognized and will probably backfire.

If you are fortunate enough to establish good leader-member relations easily, you may be reluctant to jeopardize these relations in order to have a more effective group. However, leader-member relations can become too close for effective task performance. Group members may complain about favoritism, or you may find that you cannot properly discipline a subordinate because he or she is your friend. It may then be necessary to increase the distance between your group and yourself.

For example, one Air Force commander noted that the aircraft maintenance of his unit had become sloppy. He had been having lunch and playing cards with his maintenance officers and had developed a very friendly relationship with them. He began to suspect that the maintenance officers were banking on their friendship with him to get them by with slipshod work. The commander realized that his own career would be on the line if he permitted poor work to continue.

His way of handling this problem was to gradually stop socializing with his maintenance officers. This created some concern ("Why is George no longer coming around?" "Does he still think I am doing a good job?"). These anxieties soon became translated into more careful work and greater efforts to perform good maintenance. The result was that the maintenance service markedly improved within a relatively short time. When a boss withdraws from social contact, it is difficult for the subordinate to be assured of his boss's approval in any way except by good performance.

Another officer knew he was extremely good at handling the "difficult cases," the less-motivated employees. He told his commander that he would be willing to take some of the most troublesome enlisted men in his unit, to the delight of all concerned. This made his situation more challenging and lowered his control over the situation. His performance increased and the officer was given an early promotion.

As we said earlier in Chapter 3, your relationship with your group members is the most important dimension of situational control and is, therefore, given the most weight. Changes you make in this dimension will have a greater effect on situational control than will changes in either task structure or position power. Your relationship with your subordinates is almost entirely under your own control.

Leaders are often unaware of possible changes they can make in their leader-member relations. A checklist for making such changes follows. Carefully go over this list. Some, or perhaps many, of these options may not be available to you. A few of them are almost certain to fit your situation. Make a checkmark beside each action that may be available to you.

Checklist for Changing Your Leader-Member Relations

_____ Spend more—or less—informal time with your subordinates (e.g., lunch, leisure activities, etc.).

_____ Organize some off-work group activities that include your subordinates (e.g., picnics, bowling, softball teams, excursions, etc.).

_____ Request particular people for work in your group.

_____ Volunteer to direct difficult or troublesome subordinates.

_____ Suggest or effect transfers of particular subordinates into or out of your unit.

_____ Raise morale by obtaining positive outcomes for subordinates (e.g., special bonuses, time off, attractive jobs, desirable vacation schedules).

_____ Increase or decrease your availability to subordinates (e.g., open door policy, special gripe sessions, time available for personal consultation).

_____ Share information "from above" freely with your subordinates.

Leaders have essentially two options for affecting leader-member relations. The first of these is to change the actual membership of the group. This option is very effective but is rarely available to most leaders. The second option is to increase or decrease the distance between the leader and subordinates by affecting the amount of time spent together. As is obvious from the checklist, the options suggested here for changing the leader's relations with group members are generally open to any leader who feels comfortable and effective in using them.

You may be concerned at this point whether an increase in the distance between leader and group members may not have a number of negative side-effects. Might this lower morale or job satisfaction? Would this lead to poor communication between leader and group members?

Any change a leader may make, knowingly or unknowingly, may have positive as well as negative consequences. Changes of any sort need to be made with care and with concern. However, there is no evidence that very close relations between boss and subordinate lead to good performance, or even to higher job satisfaction. Some leaders who are demanding, and closely supervise their subordinates are liked because they can make a unit effective. Others are liked because they don't bother the people they supervise.

We are certainly not recommending that you develop more distant relations with coworkers by being hostile or nasty toward them, or that you stop talking to them, or stop caring for their welfare. You may wish to recall, however, that such outstanding leaders in business and industry, as Henry Ford, Andrew Carnegie, or J. P. Morgan did not have a reputation for being cuddly. Nor were such highly respected military leaders as Generals George Patton and George Marshall, or Field Marshal Bernard Montgomery, known for their easy camaraderie with their subordinates.

MODIFYING TASK STRUCTURE

This dimension, too, permits you to modify your leadership situation to a certain degree. While the job assigned to your group may well be out of your control, you usually have some choice about how to approach your job, and how to delegate or distribute various subtasks. The following checklist suggests a number of possible steps you can take to change the structure of most tasks that come your way.

If you wish to work with a more highly structured task you can:

1. ask your supervisor to give you, whenever possible, the more structured tasks or to give you more detailed instructions;
2. learn all you can about the task so that you can prepare a detailed plan for performing the job and get additional instruction and expert guidance if needed;
3. break the job down into smaller, more highly structured subtasks;
4. volunteer for structured tasks, and avoid unstructured ones;
5. obtain further training;
6. develop procedures, guidelines, diagrams, or outlines complete with examples of previous jobs where possible.

A glance at the task structure rating scale shows that any action increasing the clarity of the job will increase structure. If you wish to work with a less structured task, you can:

1. ask your boss, whenever possible, to give you the new or unusual problems and let you figure out how to get them done;

2. bring the problems and tasks to your group members and invite them to work with you on the planning and decision-making phases of the task;
3. where possible, leave the task in relatively vague form. The ideal method of dealing with this part of the task is, of course, to work through your boss;
4. volunteer for unstructured tasks and try to avoid structured assignments.

Task structure is the second most important dimension of situational control. Be aware that changes you make in this dimension may not always be sufficient to increase or decrease situational control to the desired level. In many cases, it may be necessary to change both task structure and position power to achieve the desired effect.

Checklist for Changing Your Task Structure

Go over this list and check the options which are available to you.

1. Training

_____ Volunteer or request assignment to formal organizational training programs.

_____ Enroll in training programs outside the organization at local schools, universities, adult education, or correspondence courses.

_____ Study books or training manuals prepared by your organization.

_____ Consult books available outside the organization, such as in local libraries.

_____ Try to obtain informal training from coworkers or superiors (Is there an experienced person around who would be willing to give you some tips or background?).

_____ Approach the job in an open, unstructured way without any preconceptions.

2. Developing procedures, criteria, and feedback. The task structure rating scale makes it clear than any action increasing the clarity and specificity of procedures, criteria, and feedback will increase task structure. Listed below are some ways of accomplishing those actions.

_____ Request clearer guidelines from your supervisor.

_____ Use available expert personnel within the organizaton (e.g., expert subordinates, peers, experienced coworkers).

_____ Keep records of all aspects of the job. Attempt to increase structure by observation and systematization of regular or repeated tasks.

_____ Develop subgoals, individually or with the help of superiors, peers, and subordinates, that provide short-range criteria and feedback.

_____ Lower structure by involving a number of people with differing viewpoints to work and comment on the project. Committees are more difficult to manage, but they also provide new ideas.

3. Experience

_____ Request transfer. Frequent transfers keep the job fresh and new and do not allow extensive experience to accumulate.

_____ Decline or avoid transfers.

_____ Volunteer for long-range assignments.

_____ Make the most of experience by keeping accurate records of job-related activities.

MODIFYING POSITION POWER

While position power is defined as the power and authority the organization vests in your leadership position, there are some ways you can change your position power, although again, not all of these will work in every case.

To raise your position power, you can:

1. show your subordinates "who's boss" by exercising fully the powers that the organization provides;
2. become, as quickly as possible, an expert on the job (e.g., through training) so that you can appropriately evaluate subordinates and not have to depend on others in the group to assist you in planning and organizing the job;
3. make sure that information to your group gets channeled through you.

To lower your position power, you can:

1. try to avoid any trappings of power and rank the organization may have given you;
2. call on members of your group to participate in planning and decision-making functions. (This is essentially what participative management is about; it requires the leader to share decision making);
3. let information from the organization reach all group members as quickly and directly as possible and permit group members to know what goes on in your department and the organization;
4. let your assistants exercise relatively more power.

Position power has comparatively less weight than the other two dimensions of situational control. Changes in position power alone will often be insufficient to make a difference. You may also have to change task structure or leader-member relations to achieve the desired change in situational control.

Checklist for Changing Your Position Power

Make a check mark by those actions which may be appropriate to your situation. Position power derives primarily from organizational procedures and policies. You may not be able to change your job description or organizational policies, but subtle and effective changes are quite often very effective.

_____ Be flexible in giving rewards and punishment.
_____ Delegate authority to subordinates and allow them to share in decision making.
_____ Request aid or assistance from superiors to augment your authority.
_____ Utilize assistants to delegate some of your disciplinary responsibilities.

In trying to engineer your job you must, of course, be aware that certain changes are very difficult to undo. You cannot play the part of the "heavy" one day and the sociable, approachable boss the next day. Moreover, changes of this type should be made tentatively and in small steps so that you can gauge how far you should go for maximum effect. This is a job for a scalpel, not a meat cleaver.

It is generally unwise to make a situation deliberately very low in control. Regardless of their leadership style, leaders (especially middle LPCs) and their groups often perform less well in situations of very low leader control or very high stress than in moderate or high control situations.

The most important point, however, is to periodically reevaluate your situation after you have made adjustments to see if further fine-tuning is needed. You may find, for example, that you've made the situation too high in control, and further adjustments may be necessary. Or you may not have increased your situational control enough to improve your performance, and you may need to make additional changes.

Continuous monitoring is essential to maintain high group effectiveness. And above all, remember: Don't change your situation if you are performing effectively—

IF IT RUNS WELL, DON'T FIX IT!

PROBE 21

You are a captain commanding a city fire company. You are aware that your fire battalion chief has not been too happy with your performance in the last few months.

In analyzing your job you note that you have considerable power in assigning and disciplining people, you can recommend promotions, and your superior usually follows your recommendations. You seem to get along well with everyone and, in fact, you know that you are well liked. You also know your job well. All things considered, this is a very high control situation.

You find that you are particularly good at resolving conflict, and when the unit was new you used to be very concerned with the welfare of your group, but over the last few months you have become aloof from them. However, in the past when things have gone poorly, you talked about your problems, and sought out the people in your work group for reassurance.

1. Your leadership style is most likely to be:

    _____ relationship-motivated

    _____ task-motivated

2. As a way of increasing your performance, you could do one or more of the following:

    _____ a. Ask your battalion chief for a more difficult task to increase your job stress.

    _____ b. Ask for some of the troublemakers in the organization to be transferred to your work group.

    _____ c. Seek advice and assistance from individuals who have had longer experience in a fire company.

Feedback is given on the following page.

FEEDBACK

1. Your leadership style is probably relationship-motivated. This is indicated by your past ability to resolve conflicts and work closely with your subordinates. Your present problems with subordinates are probably the effects of extended job experience. Your experience has helped to structure the job, moving you into a very high control leadership situation.

    In such high control situations, relationship-motivated (high LPC) leaders are likely to become disinterested or self-centered and lose rapport with their subordinates. (If you had trouble with this question, review the discussion of leader types on pages 20–25, 39–40).

2. Having determined that you are relationship-motivated and you now are in a very high control situation, you would somehow want to move into a zone of moderate control, which matches your leadership style.

    One means for achieving that effect might be to ask your chief to give you a more challenging task or by taking on a difficult subordinate. You could also put yourself under greater pressure by setting tight deadlines, or developing new training methods.

    Getting advice on how to do your job would make the situation even more highly controlled and this might make your performance problem even worse.

    Job engineering is at the heart of this training program; if you had trouble with this probe, reread Chapter 9 before continuing. If you got this one right, you are doing well; try Probe 22 on the next page.

PROBE 22

You are a second-level foreman in a coal mine. You were promoted to this position after serving just nine months as a first-level supervisor. You have an LPC score of 46.

You graduated from college a year ago with course background in mining engineering. Your company likes to test future executives by giving them the kind of line experiences you now have. As a first-level foreman you had some trouble at first because your schooling included very little training in management skills. However, the work was quite technical, and after a few months things settled down and you performed quite well.

Unfortunately, your present job is much more complex and is giving you fits. There is some infighting among the foremen, who report to you, and someone always seems to be mad at you. Also, the work assignments are a lot more complex. Coordinating supplies and maintenance seems pretty hard and you have fouled up a few times.

After reading Leader Match, you feel that you are in a moderate control situation, which doesn't fit your task-motivated style. You are now considering some of the options open to you to increase your level of control.

Which of the options below might be most advantageous for you?

_____ a.   Ask your boss to transfer a couple of troublemakers into your area. The challenge might get you going.

_____ b.   Try to get assigned to a course in management communication skills.

_____ c.   Ask for a transfer at the same level to another area with different subordinates.

_____ d.   Ask your boss to give you some guidance on developing work schedules and managing materials.

_____ e.   Ask your boss to back you up on the greater use of your power, e.g., disciplining foremen with suspensions or pay cuts.

FEEDBACK

Your preferred courses of action would probably be choices (b) and (d). Training in communication skills would help you feel more comfortable in your dealings with subordinates and in managing potential conflict. Some planning advice from your boss would increase the structure and clarity of your job and give you a greater sense of control.

The other available options are less helpful. Taking on some troublemakers will decrease control even further. More stress does not seem to be what you need. A transfer is unlikely to be very useful. You would be getting right into the same kind of problem, and you will have even less familiarity with your subordinates. Although more power might increase your feelings of control a bit, you probably have sufficient power now. It's just that you aren't really sure about how to use it.

DOES SITUATIONAL CONTROL CHANGE?

We have spoken of controlling your job situation as if it were merely the result of the situation; that is, the situation provides you with control and influence to the extent to which (a) you have good relationships with your subordinates; (b) your task is structured; and (c) you have position power to direct the work of others.

A moment's reflection will tell you, however, that your situational control is likely to change over time. First of all, you typically do not step into a leadership job in which the group immediately gives you ardent support. Support usually has to be earned, and this requires time. Second, and perhaps more importantly, even the most structured task has to be learned, either by experience or by training.

This point will be readily apparent to those who have done occasional work in the kitchen. Just pick up a cookbook, and turn to soufflés or a similar recipe. The directions are all described in step-by-step detail: " . . . separate yolks and whites of six eggs . . . beat egg yolks with sugar and lemon juice until light and fluffy . . . blend in sifted flour . . . beat egg whites until stiff . . . and fold in egg yolk . . ."

Now, how do you separate yolks and whites? And what is "light and fluffy?" After you've cooked for a while you will know what these terms mean and you will learn how to perform the various operations without too much trouble. Your initial bewilderment will gradually give way to a feeling of competence. In effect, the task will have become more structured for you, and you will be less flustered and anxious as you go about following the various instructions.

A similar process occurs, of course, with nearly every new job you undertake. It takes a while to learn the ropes, and no matter how exact the instructions might be, innumerable problems require you to improvise and innovate, or to find out from others how your predecessors managed.

Clearly, then, you have less control when you begin a new job than after you have been at work for some time. As a rule of thumb, assume that a job high in control for the experienced leader will only be moderate in situational control for the inexperienced, new leader. Assume that the job moderate in control for the leader who has been on the job for some time will be low in control for the new leader.

This can be illustrated as follows:

Experienced Leader	High Control	Moderate Control	Low Control
New Leader	Moderate Control	Low Control	Extremely Low Control

Your leadership situation is a dynamic, constantly changing affair that needs careful monitoring. While you may be appropriately matched with your leadership style today, your situation may change within a month or a year, and you may find that you are not performing as well as before, or that the job is boring you and is less challenging.

Job engineering is not something you can do once and then forget. It requires constant attention and adjustment. Even if the specifications themselves do not change, your ability to deal with the job is likely to change. Generally speaking, the job is likely to become more routine over time; it will become "easier" to do, but also less challenging, thus requiring less of your attention. Your problem is to maintain a continuous balance in which your leadership style keeps matching your leadership situation.

CONSIDERING A NEW LEADERSHIP POSITION

When you are first approached with an offer to take a new leadership job, often as a promotion to a higher or more desirable position, your options are usually limited. You frequently will know less about the job than you would like to know. For example, who will be your subordinates; what kind of a person is your new boss; how much authority will you have?

Even if you are asked to move to a job you know well, declining it may mean that you will have a long time to wait before another promotion comes your way. On the other hand, you may have more leeway in making the situation fit you than first meets the eye. Let us examine the various options that might be available to you.

At best, you may be able to learn enough about the job to know that the situational control is likely to match your leadership style. In this case, of course, you should accept the new job with enthusiasm but be aware that you may become less effective as your increasing experience and knowledge on the job change the degree of control you can exercise.

You may decide that the situational control of the prospective job is a mismatch for your leadership style. Rather than risking failure, you may decline the move and explain to your boss that this is not likely to be a job in which you can do your best. This is a tough choice to make, and it usually should not be made only on the basis of the leadership situation not matching your leadership style.

Some people simply do not want to become bogged down with more administrative and managerial responsibilities. Many research scientists in charge of small teams do not want to give up their work in order to become directors of large laboratories, many teachers don't want to become principals, and some foremen don't want to become managers. In many of these cases the individual who is tapped for the job simply does not feel that he or she could be as satisfied or effective in a higher managerial position.

You may decide that you are probably mismatched for the situation for which you are slated, but that you can make a number of changes so that the job will suit you. This is a frequent case in which the candidate for the job says, in effect, "I'll take it if you will let me . . ." This will usually require an extensive discussion with your boss or with your future boss in which you explore whether you could modify certain aspects of the job (e.g., bring one of your people along as an executive assistant, report directly to Mr. X, have authority to move your immediate staff members).

It may also be possible that your job will allow you to make all the required changes informally without consulting your new boss. For example, you may arrange the work so that you create considerable distance between yourself and your subordinates by being rather formal with them, having them go through your assistant, or seeing them only by appointment. On the other hand, you may make yourself easily available, see them informally and socially, and become one of the group.

You may actively seek maximum support from your boss (for example, direct access) either as a condition of taking the job, or by keeping in close communication with him or her. Alternatively, you may decide not to lean on your boss for support, and to rely instead on yourself or the members of your group. In this case, you may want the boss to clearly define your sphere of authority. You could also bring one or more assistants with you who will give you the support you may need from immediate subordinates or, alternatively, bring in people who can play the devil's advocate.

You may, over time, change the types of jobs offered to you. This is possible in some organizations, but quite out of the question in others. However, you will almost certainly have some options in how you organize the group's task and how the task will, therefore, be structured.

Finally, you may modify your leadership situation by training, by experience, and by obtaining expert help from others in the organization. Thus, if you are a low LPC leader who has been moved into a situation of moderate control, you may increase the control by seeking relevant job training, coaching, or by breaking the tasks down into smaller, more manageable components.

One high LPC leader operating in a high-control situation adopted a participative management approach in which he shared planning and decision-making functions with his immediate subordinates. An office manager looked for a more challenging job assignment and was put in charge of evaluating and planning computerized accounting procedures for the company. Another subordinate restructured her job by training all the new members of her department.

All the strategies mentioned present certain problems. (We never said that leadership was simple!) If you only take on those jobs that best fit you, you may deprive yourself of a chance to grow in your leadership experience and to learn how to cope with new problems. You may also feel that leaders who don't take on every job, whether or not they feel particularly suited for it, are shirking their responsibility.

These are complex issues. You certainly might want to try some leadership jobs that may not be exactly suited to you just to see how you measure up to the difficulties. There is nothing wrong with this approach as long as you know what you are doing. You will certainly benefit if you carefully monitor your performance in terms of those aspects of the situation which enable you to perform well and those which cause you problems. For example, how do you perform better: if you structure the task as much as possible, or if you leave it vague and open to discussion? Do you manage better if you talk your plans over with your boss or if you play your cards close to your vest?

The second argument, that it is a moral reponsibility of the leader to tackle every problem that comes along, is a matter of conscience. Is it cowardice to duck when you are asked to do a job you know you can't handle, or is it honesty to refuse responsibilities for which you are unsuited by temperament or training? Unless you try new jobs you will not realize your full potential. If you do not perform well, your career may be in jeopardy and the organization may fail in an important mission.

On the other hand, a general practitioner surely should not undertake open-heart surgery just because he or she would feel bad about ducking the challenge. Likewise, a Navy or Army officer who volunteers for an important mission even though he might perform poorly is not doing himself or his organization a particular service. There are no simple answers for these problems and you, as every leader, will have to strike the balance that seems best to you in light of your self-knowledge and the leadership situation you face. Whatever you decide to do, it is important that you have as much information as possible to help you make an informed choice.

Apply these ideas to the following probe.

PROBE 23

Your boss has just called you in to tell you about a job opening at a higher managerial level and asks if you would like to be recommended for the job. Here are the relevant facts:

You are a low LPC leader. For the last four years you have been Department Head of the tax section of a public accounting firm and feel that you have done especially well in the last two years. The work is challenging but there are clear procedures and guidelines for most of the work.

The new job would require you to take over the entire management of your firm's regional office. This would involve supervising several department heads (e.g., Taxes, Securities, General Auditing), the office staff, as well as meeting the public to secure new business and handle public relations. You recognize that the job is much more unstructured than the one you have now. You also realize, however, that this may represent the only avenue of advancement in the firm.

Should you take the job? There is, of course, no right or wrong answer to this question. The actual choice might depend on many factors not discussed above. For example, are you content to stay in your present job? Will the organization let you? Do you have any alternative jobs that are appealing to you? What are the effects of failure?

For this exercise, let's say that you decide that you want the job. You are going to have another talk with your boss. You think that you can ask for certain conditions under which you would take the new job, but not too many. You have prepared a list of potential things to ask for, and you have decided to ask for three. Your list is shown below. Pick your three most useful actions.

_____ a. You want to pick one or two of your past subordinates to work in your new office.

_____ b. You want your new office employees to be told that the assignment is for a trial period only and may not be permanent.

_____ c. You want a three-month period in the new office to work and learn under the present manager.

_____ d. You want to be guaranteed periodic training courses both within and outside the firm.

_____ e. You want a free hand in hiring, firing, and transfer.

Feedback is given on the next page.

FEEDBACK

Assuming that you could request any of the choices, your best bets are (a), (c), and (d). Choice (a) will do much to improve your leader-member relations. You will have some people on whom you can rely and who can help to spread a positive image of you to employees who are new to you. It is, of course, important that employees already at the office are not hurt or angered by being displaced.

Another very important step is provided in choice (c). An observation and transition period under the present manager will provide considerable on-the-job training and experience. This should add an important degree of structure to the new job. Along with the training stressed in choice (d), this job should give you high control. These three measures should facilitate the match between leader and situation.

The other two possible actions have either minimal or undesirable effects. Telling your office staff that the position is temporary, choice (b), would lower your position power; having a free hand in hiring and firing, choice (e), would increase your position power. The effects of increasing power alone, however, are insufficient to move this situation to a higher zone of control.

SUMMARY

Job engineering means the modification of your leadership situation so that it matches your leadership style. Remember that the typical organization or the typical leadership situation is much more flexible than we usually realize. You can change your relations with subordinates, and your relations with superiors. You may be able to modify the structure of the task as well as the degree to which you use your position power. You can also increase your job knowledge by training and by experience.

Learning how to adjust these factors so that they fit the particular leadership style you bring to the job is perhaps one of the most important means by which you can improve your leadership performance. These same modifications also apply to your subordinate leaders, as we shall discuss in Part IV—"The Management of Managers."

PART III SELF-TEST

Listed below are several actions a manager might take to change his situational control. After reading each one, indicate whether you think the action would increase or decrease the leader's situational control.

Increase   Decrease
Control   Control

_____   _____   1. Frequently volunteer for new and different assignments.

_____   _____   2. Ask your superior to let you make all vacation and leave decisions for your subordinates.

_____   _____   3. Meet with your boss to set goals and objectives for your department.

_____   _____   4. Encourage your subordinates to make suggestions on how to accomplish job-related objectives.

_____   _____   5. Get your boss's agreement to bring into your department several subordinates with whom you have worked in the past.

_____   _____   6. Avoid close monitoring of your subordinates. Let them work on their own for relatively long periods.

_____   _____   7. Keep close records on the effect of various procedures and methods for solving problems or making decisions.

_____   _____   8. Volunteer to accept, as subordinates, employees who are trying to transfer out of other departments.

Indicate whether the statements below are true or false.

_____ 9. Relationship-motivated (high LPC) leaders perform best in low control situations.

_____ 10. Task-motivated (low LPC) leaders perform best in high and moderate control situations.

_____ 11. Low LPC (task-motivated) leaders will behave in a directive, task-focused manner in a low control situation; therefore, their performance will be relatively better than that of high LPC leaders.

_____ 12. The relationship-motivated (high LPC) leader will be anxious and tense in a low control situation, performing poorly.

_____ 13. The relationship-motivated (high LPC) leader performs best in a high control situation.

Answers to Part III Self-Test

Increase Control	Decrease Control	
	X	1. *Frequently volunteer for new and different assignments.* By changing jobs frequently, a manager does not build up experience. Thus each new job will present new, unstructured, and challenging problems to the manager.
X		2. *Ask your superior to let you make all vacation and leave decisions for your subordinates.* Having the organization give you decision power over such matters increases both your actual power and your subordinates' perception of your authority.
X		3. *Meet with your boss to set goals and objectives for your department.* Setting goals and objectives helps to clarify job demands and provides a way to assess performance, thus increasing task structure.
	X	4. *Encourage your subordinates to make suggestions on how to accomplish job-related objectives.* By asking your subordinates to make suggestions, you are automatically telling them that they have some say in the running of the department. The delegation of authority to subordinates lessens your situational control.
X		5. *Get your boss's agreement to bring into your department several subordinates with whom you have worked in the past.* This is a powerful way to improve your leader-member relations. By choosing employees with whom you have had a good working relationship, you increase the support and loyalty of your work group.
	X	6. *Avoid close monitoring of your subordinates. Let them work on their own for relatively long periods.* When you allow subordinates to work on their own, you increase their authority, and you also make it possible for a diversity of procedures to develop as each subordinate works out his or her own methods. Both of these factors serve to reduce the leader's control and to increase the challenge of the job.

Increase Control	Decrease Control	
X	_____	7. *Keep close records on the effect of various procedures and methods for solving problems or making decisions.* Good records provide structure. They allow you to assess which procedures work best and allow you to rely on these procedures for future problems.
_____	X	8. *Volunteer to accept, as subordinates, employees who are trying to transfer out of other departments.* While it may not be true in every case, you will probably receive your share of hard-to-handle employees. This will make the managing of your work group more unpredictable and, therefore, more challenging.*

False   9. *Relationship-motivated (high LPC) leaders do* **not** *perform best in low control situations.* The relationship-motivated leader performs best in *moderate* control situations.

False   10. *Task-motivated (low LPC) leaders do* **not** *perform best in high and moderate control situations.* While task-motivated leaders do perform well in a high control situation, they perform poorly in the moderate situation. It is important to distinguish between the two.

True   11. *Low LPC (task-motivated) leaders will behave in a directive, task-focused manner in a low control situation; therefore, their performance will be relatively better than that of high LPC leaders.* Task-motivated leaders do perform better than the relationship-motivated leaders in the low control situation. This is usually reflected by their task-oriented behavior.

True   12. *The relationship-motivated (high LPC) leader will be anxious and tense in a low control situation, performing poorly.* In a low control situation, relationship-motivated leaders are anxious and tense and become so concerned with seeking the support of subordinates that they do poorly at the task at hand.

*A warning is in order here. We are not suggesting that you try to take on employees who are incompetent or dangerous to the organization. Rather, it is often the case that an employee is somewhat difficult to handle but has promise as an effective worker. For example, frequently in the sports world, an athlete will perform poorly and create dissension on one team, but prove to make a very strong contribution to a new team whose coach is better able to deal with the athlete's needs.

False   13. *The relationship-motivated (high LPC) leader does* **not** *perform best in a high control situation.* The relationship-motivated leader performs best in *moderate* control situations.

By now you should have a good grasp of the things that can increase or decrease a leader's control. Examine your own job and organization and see how many of them are possible for you.

PART IV

THE MANAGEMENT OF MANAGERS

10

ENGINEERING THE LEADERSHIP SITUATION OF YOUR SUBORDINATES

Up to now we have talked about methods for improving your own leadership performance. But you probably have some subordinate leaders working for you right now—an assistant manager, a deputy, or division heads, section chiefs, etc., who report to you. If this is not the case at this time, you may either skip this chapter or else assume that you will be in that position sooner or later. Most managers do have other leaders working under their direction at one time or another, even if only temporarily, and we need to discuss your role in these circumstances. In this and the following chapter, we consider how you can assist your subordinate leaders to perform more effectively since their performance is a reflection on your own leadership.

You may find it much easier to modify your subordinates' leadership situations than your own once you have some control over (a) the types of jobs you assign them; (b) the degree to which you can give them detailed instructions or general problems; (c) the backing you provide, i.e., their position power; and (d) your relations with them. Once you identify their leadership style and the types of situations in which they perform best you are in a position to apply Leader Match at the higher management level.

The principles are, of course, well known to you by this time. You want to have leadership situations with high or low control for your task-motivated leaders, and leadership situations with moderate control for your relationship-motivated leaders.

As the boss of other leaders, you are in an excellent position to:

a. counsel them on the types of leadership situations in which they appear to perform best,

b. give them not only guidance, but also tangible assistance by modifying their leadership situation.

c. assign the leader to harmonious or to more conflicting groups, or gradually change the composition of the group to make it more harmonious or more challenging (thus increasing or decreasing leader-member relations).

d. assign to a subordinate leader either more or less structured problems and tasks to increase or decrease task structure as appropriate.

f. shore up the leader's authority by providing a great deal of support and backing, by assuring that all the organizational information is channeled through the leader, and by extending greater authority to reward and punish or by letting everyone know that you will almost certainly accept the leader's recommendations.

g. give leaders close emotional support by making yourself available to them for guidance and advice, by being as nonthreatening as possible, and by giving them assurance that you stand behind them. Alternatively, you can take a more aloof, evaluative stance, implying that subordinate leaders are on their own, and that it is up to them to find the right methods and develop appropriate policies to deal with their problems. While this latter way of dealing with your subordinate leaders might appear cold, certain types of leaders are better able to perform in this type of climate than in a warmer, more accepting atmosphere. There are also leaders who prefer this type of relationship with their boss.

As we keep emphasizing, different types of people perform better under different conditions and different levels of control. You cannot automatically assume that everyone will perform well under conditions that are optimum for you. The question of how important effective performance is to you and to your organization is, ultimately, one of value. We are not telling you that you should forego the pleasures of having close, warm relations with your subordinates. We are telling you that these pleasures, for some people, come at a price, and that it is up to you to decide whether or not you want to pay this price.

Whatever you decide to do, we must stress that you should proceed with care and caution. Small steps in a particular direction will enable you to retrace a wrong approach. Of equal importance, small steps are seen as less threatening since they permit your subordinate leaders to adjust to the changing conditions of their leadership environment. Let us now consider several other management strategies that may be open to you as a leader or manager at the second or higher level of the organization.

SELECTION AND PLACEMENT WITHIN YOUR ORGANIZATION

Job engineering is not the only method for matching a subordinate's leadership situation to his or her leadership style. You can also modify the leadership situation of your subordinate managers by a variety of other methods. One good way is selection and placement; that is, proper assignment of your subordinates to a leadership situation in which they are most likely to perform well.

Before we go any further, let us stress once more that we are talking about technically qualified leaders, that you cannot hire supervisors of aircraft designers unless they have had training in engineering, and that they should not direct an auditing department unless they are accountants. In the following discussions we are talking about leaders, or candidates for leadership positions, who are assumed to have the skills and knowledge their prospective job requires. Although the point seems obvious, our experience over the past six years suggests that it bears repetition.

Given the knowledge and skill level of the subordinate, selection and placement are, perhaps, the most obvious methods for improving the subordinate leader's performance. Yet by and large, our ability to make these assignments has not really been too successful.

The well-worn phrase that we must put round pegs into round holes and square pegs into square holes is good advice, provided the pegs and pegboards don't change their size and shape. But people and organizations are not like pegs and holes. They do change, and they change much more than we usually think.

Consider, for example, how long your own job has remained stable. How long have you had the same boss, the same key subordinates, the same tasks? In one group of thirty-two government employees working in a stable civil service system, only one manager had been in the same leadership position for more than two years—i.e., had remained with the same boss, had retained the same key subordinates, and not experienced major changes in job assignment. In most private organizations, there is even less stability over time.

Other factors also affect the situation. Have you changed your methods, have you or your boss gone to technical or management training programs? These events, also, may have made a difference in your situational control.

What does this mean for the management strategies you can adopt in selecting and placing the leaders who report to you? The answer will depend in part on whether you need someone who will perform well immediately or whether you need someone for the long run. It will also depend on how long the "long run" might be.

Does it take a few months to become an experienced hand and learn all about the job, or is this a highly complex and difficult task that might take several years to learn? In some fast food restaurant chains, first-level managers can be trained in a few days or weeks. It may take several years to train and prepare a company's production or sales manager.

If it would take several years before a manager becomes fully experienced and trained, then a "short run" strategy is more likely to pay off than waiting several years before your subordinate leader hits full stride. If, on the other hand, the leadership job can be learned in just a few months, you might be better off to pick someone who might not perform so well at first but who will become very effective within a relatively short time.

Let us say that you have a situation you diagnose as giving potentially high control to the experienced leader. This means, as we said earlier, that the job's situational control initially will be only moderate for the new leader. You, therefore, have a choice of selecting a relationship- or task-motivated leader.

If you select a relationship-motivated leader, he or she will perform well at first because relationship-motivated people perform best in moderate control situations. However, as the leader gains in experience, the situation moves into the high control condition and the relationship-motivated leader's performance will decrease.

If you select a task-motivated leader, he or she will perform rather poorly at first because task-motivated people do not perform at their best in moderate-control situations. However, as the leader gains in experience, he or she will improve and eventually overtake his or her relationship-motivated counterpart.

The opposite holds true if you initially classify the job as having moderate control for the leader. Until the leader has gained in experience and training, the situation will be low-control. Your selection problem now must involve the decision whether to go with the task-motivated leader for immediate results or with the relationship-motivated leader for the long run.

The question is whether the new manager will be of most value to your organization immediately or at some time in the future. The latter will be the case in hiring executive trainees, or someone you wish to groom for higher positions. The problem is schematically illustrated in Figure 10–1. The predicted performance of the manager is shown on the vertical axis of this graph; the zones of situational control are shown on the horizontal axis. The solid curve or line represents the relationship-motivated leader's performance; the broken line indicates the task-motivated leader's performance. As can be seen in Figure 10–1, as the relationship-motivated leader becomes more experienced in the job—as moderate control improves to high control—his or her performance is likely to *decrease*, while the task-motivated leader's performance is likely to increase. Figure 10–2 shows the relationships for task- and relationship-motivated leaders who are assigned to a moderate-control condition, which is, of course, low-control for the inexperienced leader, and then increases to moderate control as the leader obtained experience or training on

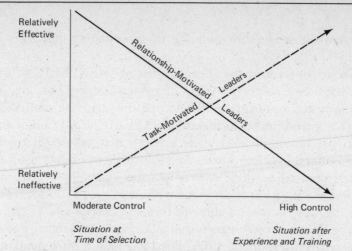

Figure 10–1 The figure illustrates a leadership situation which is very high in control for the experienced leader, and therefore only moderate for the new leader who has just been assigned to the job. This is shown on the horizontal axis across.

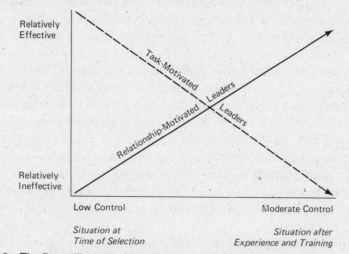

Figure 10–2 The figure illustrates a leadership situation which is moderate in control for the experienced leader, and therefore only low for the new leader who has just been assigned to the job. This is shown on the horizontal axis across.

the job. Here we find the relationship-motivated leader improving in performance, while the task-motivated leader *decreases* in performance.

The middle-LPC leader generally gains from experience and training. This type of leader will, therefore, improve in both cases—he or she will perform like the task-motivated leader shown in Figure 10–1, and like the relationship-motivated leader in Figure 10–2.

You may find it difficult to believe that increased experience and training will decrease performance for task- and relationship-motivated leaders under certain conditions. However, a number of studies under controlled conditions have shown that these effects do, in fact, occur. Thus, in a study of general managers of consumer sales cooperatives (Godfrey, Fiedler, and Hall, 1959) we identified the leadership situation of experienced managers as high in control.

When we compared the performance of INEXPERIENCED general managers with their respective high- or low-LPC scores, we found that relationship-motivated managers performed better than task-motivated leaders. When we compared the performance of EXPERIENCED general managers, we found that task-motivated leaders performed better than relationship-motivated leaders. In other words, the performance of relationship-motivated managers decreased as they gained in experience. Since the measure of performance was the ratio of net income to total sales, we know that there was actually a decrease in performance in terms of dollars and cents.

Similar findings were reported in a study of elementary and secondary school principals (McNamara, 1966, citied in Fiedler, 1978), and also of army squad leaders who were followed through an eight-month training cycle (Bons and Fiedler, 1976). These men were rated before and after the eight-month period by the same superior officers. In that case, we can be certain that the performance of relationship-motivated leaders actually showed a relative decline while that of task-motivated leaders showed a relative increase.

Chemers, Rice, Sundstrom, and Butler (1972) also showed that training decreases task performance when it results in a mismatch between leadership style and situational control. An experiment was conducted with teams of ROTC students, half of them obtaining training in deciphering simple codes, and half not obtaining this training. The situational control of the untrained group was low, that of the trained group was moderate. As the contingency model predicts, the groups led by untrained, task-motivated leaders solved more decoding tasks than did the groups led by trained task-motivated leaders, while the opposite was true of relationship-motivated leaders.

In addition, we know from everyday life that some people become bored and tired of a job they have held for too long, and they need a "challenging" (less structured) task to become effective. Some people can become over-trained, with the job no longer holding their interest. Others can stay on the same job and become better as they get more involved in its details.

As the manager of subordinate leaders you now have a number of options. Knowing the personality of your subordinates, and the nature of the task, you can select the leader who will excel at the beginning, or the type of leader who will gradually mature into a great performer.

You may require that certain leaders obtain intensive training, knowing that others may perform just as well with little or no training (again remembering that all leaders must have minimum qualifications in order to be considered for a leadership position).

You should insure that leaders are either placed in a position in which they can perform well or that the situation is modified so that their leadership potential is used to the fullest.

Thus, if you have opted for long range performance, the recommendations that might guide your procedures are indicated in Table 10–1 which follows on the next page. The general rule is that you wish to keep task-motivated leaders in high or low control situations, or get them there as soon as possible. You should keep relationship-motivated leaders in moderate control situations or get them there as soon as possible.

As the table shows, leaders newly assigned or selected for a particular situation will, of course, have less control than experienced leaders. This means that certain leaders need to be trained or coached, have their tasks structured, and their position power increased as quickly as possible. Other leaders matched to the situation as soon as they are assigned to it will gradually increase their situational control over time and must then be reassigned or rotated to a different job before becoming less effective.

Let us take, for example, a situation giving high control to the experienced leader (high LMR, high task structure, and high position power). This situation will be only moderate in control for the inexperienced leader whom you are planning to assign. Therefore:

1. Get task-motivated leaders into the high control situation as quickly as possible—e.g., provide training and coaching, structure the task, give support and high position power.
2. Keep relationship-motivated leaders (who will also be in a moderate control situation when you first assign them) in this situation as long as possible. For this reason, you do not want to increase this leader's control. Eventually you may have to rotate this leader to another job or make the job more complex in order to keep it challenging.

If you have chosen leaders for immediate, short-run results, the recommendations that might guide your procedures are shown in Table 10–1. You must first of all be aware that leaders chosen for short-term results will then not perform well if left too long on the same job. This may be a matter of months or even several years, depending on the job. Suggested strategies might be as follows:

1. Do not encourage intensive training that will quickly make the situation higher in control and less challenging, and thus decrease the leader's performance.
2. Allow your subordinate leaders to struggle with the challenge of their problems without becoming overprotective, or giving them a high degree of support. Carefully gauge how much support from you is most desirable to enable them to perform well.
3. Consider assigning new personnel periodically to the leader to keep his or her situation challenging.

Again, it is extremely important that you continually monitor and evaluate the performance of subordinate managers. This will enable you to insure the maximum effectiveness from them and allow you to make adjustments where necessary to maintain the appropriate match for your subordinate managers. Now try the probes beginning on page 210.

TABLE 10–1   Optimal Match for Effective Performance

If the situation for the experienced leader is:	The situation for the inexperienced leader is:	If the leader is:	To obtain best Long-Range Performance, proceed as follows:	To obtain best Short-Run Performance proceed as follows:
High Control	Moderate Control	Task-motivated	Train leader Structure task Increase position power Support leader	If possible, do not select If selected, train Structure task Provide position power
		Relationship-motivated	Do not increase leader control Rotate eventually	Select if possible Do not train Keep task structure low
Moderate Control	Low Control	Task-motivated	Do not increase leader control	Select if possible Do not train or structure task more than necessary
		Relationship-motivated	Train leader Structure task Support leader Increase position power, to move situation to moderate as quickly as possible	If possible, do not select If selected, train intensively, support, structure task
Low Control	Very Low Control	Task-motivated	Support leader	Select if possible
		Relationship-motivated	Structure task Increase position power Train leader	Do not select

PROBE 24

You are the manager of the Distribution Division of a book publishing house and are responsible for other distribution centers across the country. One of these branches located in a nearby city has been steadily going downhill. Book orders are not processed on time, billings are frequently mixed up, customers are irate and cancelling orders, and two shipping clerks quit in one week. Clearly a new foreman must be found as soon as possible. You are told that you can select anyone you like, but that you must produce results as quickly as possible.

In reviewing the situation you have determined that this would be a high control situation for the experienced leader: the foreman has a structured task, strong position power, and employees usually have gotten along well with him so that the leader would have maximum control. However, for a new leader, the situation initially will be only moderate in control. The new person will have to establish relations with the employees and straighten out the mess left by the previous manager. This may take as long as a year. After you screen the personnel files and recommendations of all qualified people who should be considered for the job, you find two serious candidates.

Nancy Jones has been with the company for about ten years and has been a line supervisor in production for about six of these. She is an efficient woman who has good employee relations; she is considerate but somewhat distant. Nancy runs an excellent department although when she first came to the department she seemed to have had some trouble with employees who felt that she was pushing them too hard. The division for which she is now being considered is, of course, quite different from Nancy's current job.

Bob Gomez also arrived in the company some time ago, in fact about the same time as did Nancy Jones. He had a reputation as a real winner who did a remarkable job some years ago. Recently there has been some talk that Gomez has been resting on his laurels. His performance and effectiveness leave something to be desired. His relations with employees, which were very good at first, also have deteriorated somewhat because he is seen as a little bossy and more concerned with how he gets along with his superior than with his subordinates. Whom would you choose?

_____ a.   Nancy Jones because you think she is task-motivated and this is just what you need to straighten out this mess.

_____ b.   Nancy Jones because she is relationship-motivated and she will be able to straighten the problems out in time.

_____ c.   Bob Gomez because as a task-motivated person he will tend to perform well in a difficult situation.

_____ d.   Bob Gomez because relationship-motivated people perform best in situations of this type.

Turn to the next page for feedback.

FEEDBACK

a. **You chose (a):** *Nancy Jones because you think she is task-motivated and this is just what you need to straighten out the mess.*

> This is not correct. While Nancy Jones is task-motivated, as you correctly noted, you must remember that task-motivated people in moderate control situations perform well only after they have gained experience. Until they have gained full control, task-motivated people do not perform well. In this case, you must produce results immediately, rather than with someone who will perform well only after he has been there several months or years.

Reread the section on experience on pages 20–25 and try this probe again.

b. **You chose (b):** *Nancy Jones because she is relationship-motivated and she will be able to straighten the problems out in time.*

> Your choice would indeed be correct if Nancy Jones was relationship-motivated. But you will note that Nancy was pushing people hard when she first came on the job; that is, when the situation was lower in control. Now that she is in control of the situation, she seems quite relaxed and at ease and has good, albeit distant, relations with employees. She also does a good job now in this situation which is surely very high control. These are all marks of the task-motivated leader.

Reread the section describing relationship- and task-motivated people (pages 203–208) again, and then try this probe again.

c. **You chose (c):** *Bob Gomez because task-motivated people perform well in a difficult situation.*

> You are correct in your belief that task-motivated leaders perform best in difficult situations, but you missed the boat on two major counts:
> 1. Bob Gomez is relationship-motivated. His relations with employees were good at first, and he also performed very well when he started his job, but he has been less effective lately. He has also become less concerned with his leader-member relations. All this points to relationship-motivation rather than task-motivation.
> 2. Even though the Distribution Division is a mess, this is not a low control situation. As you recall, it is a moderate control situation. A relationship-motivated leader would, of course, perform best under these conditions.

Reread the section on diagnosing the control of situations in Chapter 7 and also the section on diagnosing personality of leaders in Chapter 2. Then make another choice of the alternatives given in Probe 24.

d. **You chose (d):** *Bob Gomez because relationship-motivated people perform best in situations of this type.*

> This is the correct choice. Bob Gomez is a relationship-motivated leader: He performed well at first and then gradually went downhill as his training and experience made the situation higher in control.
>
> Also, his relationship with his subordinates shows the pattern typical of a relationship-motivated leader, i.e., in a high-control situation, the leader becomes less considerate and more aloof from subordinates. This new job as head of the Distribution Division, is likely to be a moderate control situation for a new leader. Thus, a relationship-motivated leader would perform well at first. Bob Gomez would seem to be the right person for that job, as you correctly indicated.

Go on to Probe 25.

PROBE 25

You are an executive of an oil company with many foreign installations. Your company has a contract to build a new base in a remote area of an Arab country. Most project workers will be local Arab personnel with a few American technicians. You must pick someone to head the field team. He will be in charge of the entire operation which involves the construction of an oil exploration and drilling base and the development of procedures to make the base operational. You will be able to give the person you choose some culture training which should give him some knowledge of what cultural patterns might affect the work.

You have the following personnel from which to pick your manager. Whom would you choose?

_____ a. Charles Meecham. An experienced relationship-motivated engineer with specific training in base construction.

_____ b. Sam Kennedy. A brilliant young task-motivated engineer with very little experience.

_____ c. Roy Stewart. A bright relationship-motivated engineer. Very little experience.

_____ d. Nick Foster. A highly experienced task-motivated engineer, trained in base design and maintenance.

Go to the following page for feedback.

FEEDBACK

This was a difficult item, which had many facets and required considerable thought—in other words, a typical leadership problem.

Your first thought should have been to figure out the situational control of the job. Building an oil base in a foreign country with a culturally mixed work force could not even come close to being a high control situation. It is probably moderate for a trained and experienced man and very low for an untrained person. The cultural training might take some of the conflict out of the culturally mixed group, and improve leader-member relations somewhat. The field manager will have high position power.

Here we threw you another curve. Basing a decision only on the theory presented in this manual, you could choose either the experienced Charles Meecham or the inexperienced Sam Kennedy. While both of these choices fit the theory, (i.e., Meecham is a relationship-motivated leader whose experience makes the situation moderate in control, and Kennedy, a task-motivated leader whose lack of experience makes the situation low in control), they are obviously not equally good in practice. One must feel extremely hesitant to send a young and inexperienced person on such a difficult job. Charles Meecham is, therefore, the better choice.

This exercise helps to illustrate an important point made in the introduction. This program will augment sound management thinking, not replace it. An executive would surely want to send a trained and experienced person to head an important project in the field. The method detailed here helps the executive select which person is likely to have the most effective leadership pattern.

PROBE 26

Mike Sampson is a young civil engineer who was recently hired as a first line supervisor in your department—he is still quite inexperienced. Mike came very highly recommended, is highly intelligent, and very well motivated. You place him in charge of a construction crew to build a typical logging road into a wilderness area. While the men seem to like him moderately well, his performance has been quite disappointing and his crew is behind schedule. When the work is not going too well (which has happened quite a lot lately) he more or less locks himself into his office, works on new plans and procedures and spends very little time with his men.

   You need to take some action to remedy the situation to see if his performance can be improved. Mike's LPC score is 44. He has been on the job about six months and still seems very nervous about doing well. The company has no special training program for this rough (but quite routine) kind of road building. You have listed below several possible actions that you might take. Check the best course (or courses) of action.

_____ a.   Tell Mike that his performance is poor and give him a reasonable time period (say three months) to improve performance or be replaced.

_____ b.   Introduce Mike to one of the older, more experienced supervisors and ask this person to give him a few pointers.

_____ c.   Sit down with Mike and try to plan out some short-range goals and some guidelines for building logging roads. This should improve his task structure somewhat.

_____ d.   Give Mike a new assignment with a chance to demonstrate how creative he can be.

_____ e.   Suggest to Mike that he spend more time getting to know his crew and gaining their support and confidence.

Turn to the next page for feedback.

FEEDBACK

Choices (b), (c), and (e) represent possible solutions to Mike's problem. Mike is a low LPC, or task-motivated, leader. He is new to the job and probably does not yet know and understand exactly what to do. Thus, the situation is moderate in control. Because Mike is probably pressing too hard his performance is suffering. The best course of action involves taking steps to increase his control of the situation until it better matches Mike's leadership style.

Choices (b) and (c) both involve increasing task structure. In one case this is done through informal training by an experienced person and in the other by providing task structure from his superior. By itself, increased structure is probably not enough to move his job into a higher zone. So choice (e), perhaps in combination with (c), may be the best selection because it involves leader-member relations, which is the most important dimension. Changing both leader-member relations and task structure, however, should definitely improve Mike's situation.

Choices (a) and (d) would decrease Mike's control by adding stress or decreasing task structure. Neither course of action is warranted. It is true that the situation could change enough to become a low-control situation, and that Mike's performance might improve somewhat. As we have said earlier, however, this is a dangerous and potentially poor course of action. Very low control situations often tend to be quite volatile and do not represent a stable, productive situation.

Be sure to reevaluate situations of this type in a few weeks to see if your changes have improved the leader's performance.

If you got this one right—you are on your way! Now try Probe 27.

If you missed this one, you should review Chapter 3 on determining situational control.

PROBE 27

You are President of an architectural engineering firm. You have recently hired a young engineer, Jack Meyer, to direct the bridge design section of your firm. He is a brilliant young man who should be a strong addition to your firm. He is a low LPC leader.

Meyer's job as head of the bridge section is to direct the work of several engineers and draftsmen who design or draft portions of larger projects. The work of his subordinates is reasonably well structured. They work within specifiable limits with fairly standard procedures. Several of these men are older and more experienced but less talented than their leader. They like him well enough but are not really sure that he should be their boss.

Your problem is that Meyer's department's performance has been relatively poor and is costing the company money in terms of overtime and penalties. In addition, he has been using strong discipline to get the department moving. This does not work very well, especially since company structure gives the section leader no real power to hire or fire people. Authority for hiring as well as salaries and promotion are centered in the personnel department and higher management levels. The situational control is likely to be moderate.

Listed below are courses of action that might have the effect of improving performance in the bridge department. Choose those you think are most appropriate to the present situation.

_____ a.   Change the personnel of his unit so that it will be more difficult for him to get to know his staff.

_____ b.   Start taking actions designed to improve Meyer's authority and position; e.g., channel all information through him, include him in meetings at higher levels, make it clear that his suggestions carry weight.

_____ c.   Provide Meyer with intensive training and guidance.

_____ d.   Transfer him to a new job, and keep moving him around so that his job remains exciting and challenging.

_____ e.   Fire him. His performance indicates that the high expectations for him were in error.

_____ f.   Leave him alone. Things will probably get better eventually.

_____ g.   Allow him to add a couple of men of his own choice to his department.

The next page will give you feedback on your choices.

FEEDBACK

Jack Meyer is in a moderate control situation, a position appropriate for a high LPC leader. Meyer is, however, a low LPC leader, and therein lies the problem.

An evaluation of various alternatives is given below:

a. *Change the personnel of his unit so it will be more difficult for him to get to know his staff.*

This might lower the situational control to an area more suitable for a low LPC leader.

This course of action would probably be unwise for two reasons. First, in general it is a bad idea to push a leadership situation into low control regardless of leadership style. Groups in such a situation frequently show a general decrease in performance. Second, as Meyer became more experienced the structure of his job would increase, carrying him back into an inappropriate level of situational control.

b. *Start taking actions designed to improve Meyer's authority and position.*

This would be a useful but not sufficient course of action. Improving his power would move the situation closer to high control. However, since position power is the weakest of the three situational dimensions, this action alone would probably not be enough.

c. *Provide Meyer with intensive training and guidance.*

This would be a good course of action. Providing him with training would have the same effect as giving him a more structured task. This would be a major step in moving his situation into a high control zone, best suited to his leadership orientation.

d. *Transfer him to a new job.*

This action is contraindicated. Moving him around would have the effect of maintaining an unstructured and ambiguous task environment, which is the last thing he needs.

e. *Fire him.*

This action would be premature. From what we know about situational effects on leadership performance, it would be unwise to dismiss a talented and potentially useful manager without attempting to salvage his talents.

f. *Leave him alone.*

This is a possible option. Experience and stability will eventually improve the situation enough to improve Meyer's performance. However, the company probably cannot afford to wait that long.

g. *Allow him to choose some new subordinates.*
    This would be a positive step. It would allow Meyer to improve the
    support of subordinates by bringing in some people he can work with, and
    possibly showing others that he can be a good man to work for. This could
    also backfire, causing further alienation among his subordinates in the
    bridge department.

SUMMARY

This chapter dealt with engineering your subordinate managers' jobs, and with leadership selection and placement, stressing that control of the situation changes as the leader gains in experience on a particular job. Therefore, we cannot merely place a task-motivated leader in high or low control situations, and a relationship-motivated leader in a moderate control situation. Rather, we must consider that new leaders will experience the situation as lower in control until they have established themselves as trustworthy with their group members, and until they have learned the task fully.

The time it takes for a leader to reach his or her full level of experience will vary according to the job. Leaders assigned to relatively simple tasks will take less time than those assigned to very complex and difficult tasks. Leaders given extensive training will take less time than those given none. And leaders assigned to "difficult" groups will take longer to develop good leader-member relations (if they can do so at all) than will leaders assigned to congenial, highly homogeneous groups.

Sound strategy calls for the selection and placement of leaders by long-run and short-run needs. Choose leaders whose best performance is required immediately but who can be expected to become less effective over time, or leaders who may perform rather poorly at first but who will become increasingly better as the situation begins to match their personality.

The basic strategies for various conditions of situational control are shown in the Table 10–1 on page 209.

Chapter 11 describes how to apply these concepts to rotation and transfer.

11

ROTATION AND TRANSFER

Moving from one job to another is part of organizational life in many business and industrial concerns, as well as in many governmental agencies. If these moves are made as particular jobs need to be filled, and if they are primarily for the benefit of the organization, they are usually called transfers. When the moves are part of a systematic policy calling for periodic reassignments to broaden the leader's experience and perspective, they are considered part of a rotation program.

Whatever their reason for moving, very few managers in large companies, or leaders in the military services, remain in the same position for more than a few years. Very little is known about the effects that rotation and transfer might have on the effectiveness of the individual or of his or her organizational unit.

The general assumption has been that it must be good for the organization and for the leader since it broadens managers' perspectives and provides cross-fertilization. Whether it is good for everyone under all conditions depends on the use managers are able to make of this broadening experience. The evidence is far from clear. Let us here consider the effects of transfers and rotation in light of this training program. What are the likely results of changing jobs, and of a high turnover of one's own superiors or subordinates on managerial effectiveness?

While managerial rotation is generally seen as beneficial, "organizational turbulence," (that is, rapid and unsystematic turnover among subordinates, changes in job requirement, changes in higher managers, and economic upheaval) is seen as disruptive and as leading to poorer performance. Upon closer inspection, the factors affecting leaders in their day-to-day interactions with their boss, subordinates, and peers are identical, whether we talk about rotation, transfer, promotion, or turbulence. In each of these cases you, as the leader, must learn to adjust to major changes in the situation.

What specific elements change? A change of boss requires leaders to learn the new superior's standards and expectations, including any idiosyncracies that must be considered. Most leaders and their new bosses do manage to adjust to each other. This may take a few months or a few years, but until the relationship stabilizes, the leader must live with a certain amount of anxiety and insecurity.

Similarly, for a certain amount of time newly transferred leaders will not be able to trust their new subordinates. Do they really know that they are doing? Can they be relied upon to do the job right? If the leader gets into trouble, will they support him? Who in the group are the key people who need to be won over if changes are to be made?

Finally, leaders must learn what the new job is all about. What must they know about the work itself? How is it done in the new place, how do they look for problems, how do they get things fixed, who are the experts in the organization on whom they must depend, and to whom should they turn for help? Whom should they see if they run into trouble with suppliers, customers, or other managers at the same level of the organization? Above all, who are the real powers, the people to see if you want to get something done? Or the people who can damage your standing in the organization?

These are all-important questions whether or not the move was made for the purposes of rotation or promotion, or whether the effects came about because of so-called organizational turbulence. Practically all of these questions lower the leaders' control. One major exception might be, for example, a move by a leader from a low control situation to a new job involving more control—e.g., from being the disliked manager of an advertising department to a well-liked director of a production department. Since most rotations and transfers change the situation, these moves should correspondingly improve the performance of some leaders but decrease the performance of others.

Staying on the same job too long may result in lower performance on the part of some people. They become stale or bored with the job, no longer interested and challenged by the problems they must tackle, and no longer as motivated as they were at first. Others, however, will like the continuity, and improve their performance on the job. Again, different people obviously have different goals as well as different strengths and weaknesses as managers.

Consider, for example, your best managerial troubleshooter who is sent out to fight "brushfires." If you leave this person at the same branch office or trouble spot so long that there are no more fires to extinguish or problems to solve, he or she is likely to become bored and disinterested. There is no more challenge and this person will now either stir up trouble—which you don't need—or pay less attention to the job and become correspondingly less effective.

Other people simply need more time to become maximally effective. They take pride in learning their job inside-out. And some managers are cut out for the day-to-day administration of departments or plants, and do this superbly. But the same people frequently are less able to handle conflict. Therefore, rotation and transfer should take into consideration the individual's leadership style as well as situational control if effectiveness and performance of the organizational unit is important.

THE BEST TIME TO ROTATE OR TRANSFER

In principle, the best time to move a manager to another job comes when the high LPC leader, by virtue of his or her experience and training, is no longer working in a moderate control situation, or the low LPC leader is no longer working in a high or low control situation.

Accurate diagnosis is essential here. You must know not only the personality and leadership style of your subordinate leaders, but also the amount of control of the situation. However, you must also maintain a careful record of leader performance. When the performance of a leader or manager begins to slip, even though the person did an excellent job earlier, then it is time to consider whether the job has become too routine or too structured, or else too vague or stressful. Does the work no longer offer sufficient challenge to meet the leader's needs, or has it changed in the direction of being too challenging for the particular person? You must then decide whether to attempt to engineer the job as we discussed earlier, or if that isn't possible, to rotate or transfer.

In general terms, it will be useful for you to collect information about the relationship of time on the job to the amount of situational control for all positions under your direction, or else you will have to make an educated guess. Based on your knowledge of the job, you might be able to estimate the amount of time it takes for a manager to become experienced, or to increase situational control as a result of experience.

Your informal observations will usually tell you a good deal. How many months or years does it take until a person in a particular leadership job is no longer considered "new" or "inexperienced?" When does he or she become "an old hand"; that is, someone to whom others turn for advice? You might also ask how long the average manager or leader remains in a particular job. Institutional wisdom and practice frequently are good indicators as to the peak effectiveness of a managerial job. Thus, if most managers remain at the division manager level for four years before being moved up or out, the optimum time of managerial experience is likely to be around two or three years, with some managers becoming notably restless and less effective and others beginning to hit their stride.

A more systematic way to gauge this relationship may be possible. If, for example, you have a sizable number of leaders who have similar positions but varying job tenure, you could have them fill out the rating forms for the positions. From the situational control data you obtain in this manner, you will then be able to determine the average amount of job experience required before a manager moves into the next higher zone of situational control.

Whether you make a systematic survey or only an educated guess, there is no substitute for carefully maintained performance evaluations. We cannot overemphasize the point that good performance records and evaluations are invaluable assets for an organization wanting to develop and keep a well-performing pool of leadership and managerial talent.

Now try the probe on the following page.

PROBE 28

You are the general manager of an assembly plant. Company policy requires the periodic rotation of managers, generally every four years. However, you know that certain people need more or less time to reach their maximum performance levels.

Tim Caldwell, one of your division managers, has been on the job for 37 months. The division he heads deals with engineering and maintenance problems, a highly structured task. Caldwell started off very well. His relations with his men were excellent, he was enthusiastic about the job, and he liked to tackle new problems. He is known as an approachable and sociable person. Several months ago his relations with his men began to deteriorate. You have the feeling that he is trying to impress you, and that he is no longer involved with the work itself.

How would you diagnose the problem?

a. Caldwell is a low LPC person who needs to be transferred to a new job that is more highly structured.

b. Caldwell is a high LPC person, and what you see is simply the consequence of his "moving" from a moderate to a high control situation. You therefore rotate him to a new job of moderate control.

c. Caldwell is low LPC. His situation was low in control to begin with, and it has become moderate. He therefore needs another low control situation, and you plan to change his job to that of troubleshooter for the design section.

d. Caldwell is high LPC, and you decide that he needs to remain on the job until he gets his feet back on the ground. You figure that he would do best if you gave him a smaller unit since he is good at supervising this type of work.

FEEDBACK

a. **You choose (a):**   *Caldwell is a low LPC person who needs to be transferred to a new job which is more highly structured. This is incorrect.*

> All indications are that you are dealing with a high LPC person. His good performance at the beginning of his job as well as his good relations with subordinates at that time point to this conclusion. Likewise, the fact that Caldwell is trying to develop good relations with you rather than with his subordinates is characteristic of a high LPC leader in a high control situation. Remember that high LPC leaders become inconsiderate of their subordinates if the situation is too high in control. Caldwell's situation appears to be high control now that he had been on the job for quite some time. He has position power and has a structured task. His relations with his subordinates are fairly good although perhaps not quite as good as they were at the beginning.

You missed on this one. Review the first few chapters and then try this probe again.

b. **You chose (b):**   *Caldwell is a high LPC person, and what you see is simply the consequence of his "moving" from a moderate control to a high control situation. You therefore rotate him to a new job of moderate control.*

> This is correct on both counts. You should rotate Caldwell to a situation which is moderate control for a new leader. This might well be a task which, after an appropriate time interval, might become high control. But for the moment, you are best off with Caldwell in a job that challenges him.
>
> It would probably be unwise to assign him to a job that is unstructured, has low position power and possibly poor leader-member relations (that is, a situation likely to be low control), in the expectation that he will in time and with experience have a moderate control leadership situation. You are better off considering him for a job that is moderate in control right now.

c. **You chose (c):**   *Caldwell is a low LPC. His situation was low in control to begin with, and it has become moderate. He therefore needs another low control situation and you plan to change his job to that of troubleshooter for the design section.*

> This is not correct. The brief description of Caldwell's relations with his subordinates indicates that he is probably a high LPC person. He was friendly and approachable at first, but his relationships deteriorated over

time and he began to seek a closer relationship with the boss. This is a pattern typical of high LPC persons.

Note also that he deals with a highly structured task. It is unlikely that this situation was ever low in control. It was probably of moderate control for a new leader and became high in control as the leader gained experience.

Rethink this probe and make another choice.

d. **You chose (d)**: *Caldwell is high LPC, and you decide that he needs to remain on the job until he gets his feet back on the ground. You figure that he would do best if you gave him a smaller unit since he is good at supervising this type of work.*

We have some good news and some bad news. The good news is that you accurately assessed Caldwell's leadership style. The bad news is that your plan of action is likely to make his performance even worse.

Caldwell's problem appears to stem from the fact that his 37 months of experience made his job too structured, and he has lost interest and motivation. The solution is not to increase his control further, as would be the result if you leave him on the same job and give him very structured responsibilities. Rather, he should be given a job better suited to his leadership motivation; that is, one less structured.

Consider the alternatives, and make another choice.

SUMMARY

Leadership situations change over time, as do the knowledge and abilities a leader brings to a task. As the leader gains in experience, ability, and job knowledge, each leadership assignment will become more routine and less challenging.

One important method for increasing the challenge of the job involves decreasing the leader's situational control by systematic rotation of the manager to another job. Keeping good performance records will help you to judge the most appropriate time for rotating or transferring a subordinate leader.

Now try the Part IV Self-Test on the next page.

PART IV SELF-TEST

Select the statement that best completes or answers each item below.

_____ 1. The largest and most dramatic changes in engineering leadership situations for subordinates will result from actions affecting:
   a. Leader-member relations
   b. Task structure
   c. Position power
   d. Overall situational control

_____ 2. You are selecting a manager to direct the operation of a bookkeeping department with fairly routine procedures and responsibilities. Leader-member relations should be quite good, and position power is high. You need immediate performance at a high level. What type of leader would you select?
   a. Low LPC, task-motivated
   b. High LPC, relationship-motivated

_____ 3. You are selecting a manager for your firm's extensive public relations functions. Morale is good, but the job is extremely unstructured. You are primarily concerned with high level performance over the long run. What type of leader would you choose?
   a. Low LPC, task-motivated
   b. High LPC, relationship-motivated

_____ 4. The effect of job rotation on situational control is:
   a. Generally to increase control
   b. Generally to decrease control
   c. Generally to not affect control

_____ 5. You have a subordinate manager who is a low LPC, task-motivated leader. She is presently in a situation of moderate control and is performing poorly. Which of the following courses of action is best?
   a. Increase the pressure on her, tighten deadlines, and become personally aloof.
   b. Provide her with better guidelines, more frequent feedback, and a better feeling of support from the organization.
   c. Assign the manager to some extensive training courses, while you withdraw, become more aloof, and demand higher performance.
   d. Do nothing.

Answers to Part IV Self-Test

___a___ 1. *The largest and most dramatic changes in engineering leadership situations for subordinates will result from actions affecting:* Leader-member relations. Leader-member relations are the single most important factor affecting the leader's control. Changes in group composition or in organizational support for the leader can drastically change the leader's situational control.

___b___ 2. *You are selecting a manager to direct the operation of a bookkeeping department with fairly routine procedures and responsibilities. You need immediate performance at a high level. What type of leader would you select?* High LPC, relationship-motivated. This situation has the potential to be fairly highly structured. However, it would be relatively low in structure for a new leader. Assuming leader-member relations to be reasonably positive, this position is likely to be of moderate situational control for the new manager. A high LPC leader should deliver high performance in the short run.

___b___ 3. *You are selecting a manager for your firm's extensive public relations functions. Morale is good, but the job is extremely unstructured. You are primarily concerned with high level performance over the long run. What type of leader would you choose?* High LPC, relationship-motivated. In this question you must be sensitive to the long run potential for structure and control. Given the extremely unstructured nature of public relations, even extensive time on the job should not make the task very structured. Thus, even in the long run, the job promises to be one of moderate control calling for a relationship-motivated person.

___b___ 4. *The effect of job rotation on situational control is:* Generally to decrease control. Job rotation is a systematic change in leadership positions. The high rate of change makes it impossible to gain experience which would add structure and control. Thus, by restricting opportunities to gain experience, rotation effectively decreases control.

___b___ 5. *You have a subordinate manager who is a low LPC, task-motivated leader. She is presently in a situation of moderate control and is performing poorly. Which of the following courses of action is best?* Provide her with better guidelines, more frequent feedback, and a better feeling of support from the organization.

12

CAPITALIZING ON YOUR JOB-RELEVANT ABILITIES

In this chapter, we temporarily switch to a somewhat different topic. As you undoubtedly recognize, your leadership style and its match with the situation, important as they may be, are not the only factors determining your performance. When we hire someone for a managerial job, or start working with someone, we almost invariably give some thought to how bright this person may be and how much experience he or she may have for the job. Very few executives deliberately try to hire dull and inexperienced managers. By the same token, we want the managers we do hire to use their heads (their intellectual abilities) and the knowledge they have acquired in their jobs.

But people do not always use their heads, and there probably have been times when you felt you "should have known better" than to do or not to do something. How can you make sure that you do make good use of your intellectual abilities and your experience?

The problem again turns out to be one of matching your situation to your personal abilities and attributes. For most people, being brighter or more experienced than others does not, by itself, guarantee that they will be better leaders.

We have been neglecting the middle-LPC leaders up to this point. However, when it comes to making good use of their abilities and the knowledge they have gained from their experience, the middle LPC leaders clearly seem to have the edge. They are less concerned with their role as a supervisor, and less easily disturbed by what others think of them. For this reason they do not tend to get as easily involved in interpersonal problems that are emotionally draining and would keep them from thinking about anything else. By and large, therefore, if you are a middle LPC person, your intellectual abilities and the knowledge you gained from your job experience and training are likely to help you in most leadership situations. High and low LPC leaders need to be aware of the fact that they use their intellectual abilities and their experience much more effectively under some conditions than others. The problem of making good use of your abilities and your know-how is very real.

You can look around almost any organization and find some extremely bright people who have failed as managers, while some not so bright people have been highly effective. A leader who is not unusually intelligent may have the ability to inspire people, to motivate them, to give them confidence in his or her integrity, and in his or her concern for their welfare.

In fact, some very bright leaders might be seen as the "know-it-alls" who never listen to anyone else before charging ahead and messing things up. They also include the managers who get so involved trying to see all the angles and understand all the options that they become immobilized and have a hard time getting on with the job. On the other hand, of course, there are many bright leaders who perform extremely well, who really do use their heads.

The principle is, of course, "If you've got it, use it!" What are the conditions under which you can best capitalize on your intellectual abilities if you fall into the bright group?

You obviously have to be honest about yourself and about your intellectual abilities. Not everybody is a genius, and not everybody needs to be one.

All of us would like to think that we are brighter than others in the group we compare ourselves with. But it is mathematically impossible. Not all of us can be brighter than the average, and it's important to know into which group you happen to fall. Since most people do not even come close to effectively making use of what they do have, even the less well-endowed leaders who make effective use of their abilities are likely to be well ahead of the crowd.

If you are a first line supervisor or manager, the chances are good that you are somewhat brighter than most of your group members. If you are at the second or third level of management, you can take it for granted that you are considerably brighter than the average citizen. The important question is, however, whether you have a higher intelligence level than the average of the managers with whom you are compared, or with whom you compete.

To give an example from outside management, college professors, as a group, have very high IQs (average about 125–130). The job demands it, and the educational system, with its many examinations, screens out those who are not intellectually able to handle the jobs of teaching and research. But some are clearly brighter than others; that is, brighter than the job requires as a minimum, although they are not necessarily more effective. A lot of bright people are disorganized and spin their wheels. We are concerned with helping you to use what you have, not what you'd like to have.

So, whether or not you happen to be especially bright, let's take a look at how you can best use what you have at your disposal. You first have to ask yourself three questions and answer them with brutal honesty:

1. HOW DO YOU COMPARE WITH OTHERS IN YOUR GROUP?

Compared to others in your line of work, and your level at the organization, how intelligent are you? Here are a few landmarks that might help you with your answer:

Y   N   a.   Are you usually able to see problems before others in your peer group see them?

Y   N   b.   Are you quicker to understand instructions and new policies than others in your group?

Y   N   c.   Do other managers often come to you for explanations of technical problems, instructions, directives, policies, or new legislation explained to all of them verbally or in writing? Do they ask you more often than you ask them?

Y   N   d.   When a new problem comes up, can you usually see its relationship to other problems, while others have a hard time seeing these connections?

Y   N   e.   Do you often wonder why your peers cannot see or understand something that seems perfectly obvious to you?

Number YES Answers _____
Number NO Answers _____

If you have answered most of these questions with YES, the chances are that you are brighter than most people in your group. If you answered most questions with a NO, don't worry about it. As we said before, you don't need to be a genius to be an outstanding leader. General Eisenhower and Field Marshall Montgomery, two of World War II's greatest leaders, were bright, but reputedly less so than others at their level.

2. DO YOU HAVE A STRESSFUL RELATIONSHIP WITH YOUR BOSS?

The second question you have to ask yourself concerns your relationship with your immediate boss (although a very stressful relationship with your group members will have a similar effect). The simplest way to go about this is to mark

the scales shown below by checking the point on the scale that best describes
your relationship with your boss:

Relaxed ____:____:____:____:____:____:____:____Very
easy   8   7   6   5   4   3   2   1   stressful

   a. Does the boss often pressure you to do more than you can reason-
      ably accomplish?

Definitely____:____:____:____:____:____:____:____Definitely
true   8   7   6   5   4   3   2   1   not true

   b. Does the boss give you so little information that you often don't
      know what you are supposed to do?

Definitely____:____:____:____:____:____:____:____Definitely
not True   1   2   3   4   5   6   7   8   True

   c. When you get a difficult job, does the boss usually have the
      attitude that that's your tough luck, and let you struggle on your
      own, even if he or she could help you by giving you additional
      information, personnel, or equipment?

Definitely____:____:____:____:____:____:____:____Definitely
True   8   7   6   5   4   3   2   1   not True

   d. Do you often feel that you could do your job a lot better if your boss
      would only let you do it your own way?

Definitely____:____:____:____:____:____:____:____Definitely
not True   1   2   3   4   5   6   7   8   True

   e. Do you feel that your boss meddles in your group, and in the way
      you want your subordinates to do their job?

Definitely____:____:____:____:____:____:____:____Definitely
True   8   7   6   5   4   3   2   1   not True

If you answered most of these questions in the positive, you have a very
stressful relationship with your boss. UNDER THESE CONDITIONS, YOU
WILL FIND IT DIFFICULT IF NOT IMPOSSIBLE TO MAKE GOOD
USE OF YOUR SUPERIOR INTELLECTUAL ABILITIES. YOU WILL
NEED TO CHANGE THE RELATIONSHIP WITH YOUR BOSS. We'll talk
about some ways of doing so later in this chapter.

3. WHAT DOES THE TASK DEMAND?

Our third question concerns the nature of the task. You must capitalize on what
you have—on your strength, not on your weakness, or what you would like to

have. Intelligent people shine in jobs requiring intellectual ability, not necessarily in jobs requiring athletic ability or the ability to handle difficult interpersonal relations.

Athletic people shine in jobs requiring athletic ability. People who are interpersonally sensitive and tactful shine in jobs that require interpersonal tact and sensitivity, and not necessarily in jobs requiring athletic prowess or intellectual ability. If you are highly intelligent, it makes sense that you seek leadership jobs that require a high degree of intellectual ability. If that is not your forte, stay away from these jobs.

What kinds of jobs call for intellectual ability? Rate your job on the degree to which it requires the following, by distributing 100 points among the 10 leadership functions are listed below:

_____ a.   planning and organizing the work of others
_____ b.   advising the boss on policy issues or problems
_____ c.   supervising personnel
_____ d.   inspecting and evaluating the operation of various units
_____ e.   developing new methods, techniques, or policies
_____ f.   analyzing and interpreting data on sales, production, overhead, etc.
_____ g.   writing reports, advertising copy, letters
_____ h.   dealing with difficult employees, customers, other managers
_____ i.   supervising sales, bookkeeping, production departments employing nonmanagerial employees
_____ j.   supervising and coordinating the work of supervisory and managerial employees

If you allotted the majority of points to items a, b, e, and/or f, your job is intellectually demanding. The scale is, of course, only a guide. You may have a job not covered by the 10 functions we listed, one requiring a lot of intellectual effort—e.g., supervising investigations of patent infringements or fraudulent accounting, or, presiding over an administrative court. Needless to say, it is important that you do not kid yourself into thinking that your job is more intellectually demanding than it really is.

WHAT, THEN ARE THE BASIC GROUND RULES?

1. You can use your intellectual abilities to advantage only if your relationship with your boss is relatively free of stress. If you have stressful relations with your boss, you probably will not be able to use your intellectual abilities to advantage. You must change your relationship with your boss before you do anything else. How do you do this?

a. First, take careful note of the specific things your boss says or does that cause you to feel stress and anxiety. Is it his or her aloofness, the constant demand for getting things done quickly, getting work piled on too fast, or that you never seem to do things well enough?

b. Identify when the stress is likely to occur. For example, does your boss cause you stress more often in the morning when there is a lot of stuff coming into the office, or in the evening when people are tired and the day's deadlines are still to be met?

Do you feel more stress when you see the boss alone or when you see the boss at staff meetings or at social occasions? Is there more stress when a job is insufficiently explained to you, or does the stress come from the feeling that you can never do things right? Other questions of this type will occur to you.

WHAT CAN YOU DO ABOUT THIS?

There is usually something you can do to avoid these stresses.

1. You can for example, try to see your boss earlier in the day when both of you are not tired, or later in the day, when things have calmed down.

2. You can try to avoid eyeball-to-eyeball confrontations by telephoning or writing memos rather than seeing the boss personally.

3. You can carefully plan what you will say to your boss rather than trying to ad lib at the last moment, and you can do your "homework" well before meeting with the boss.

4. You can desensitize yourself to the stress in your relationship with your boss to some extent by visualizing yourself in various stress-producing situations with the boss.

5. You can role-play difficult interviews you anticipate with your boss by getting your spouse, a friend, or a coworker, to play the boss's part.
     For further guidance on stress management see various books on the topic, or take stress management training.

6. Above all, you must learn how to let your boss know the conditions under which you work best.

a. First, take careful note of the things your boss does that cause you to feel less stressed and more comfortable. (Surely, not everything he or she does causes you stress!)

b. The next time your boss shows one of these behaviors, say something nice and complimentary. You don't have to fear in the slightest that it will be resented. Bosses are as hungry for compliments and bouquets as anyone, and they receive them all too rarely from their subordinates.

If your boss gives you some help, be effusive but sincere in your praise. Say, for example, "Gee, boss, it's really nice of you to give me a hand with this problem. Now I know how it should be done," or, "You know, I really appreciate it when you tell me exactly how you want me to handle this. This way, I feel I can do a better job."

REDESIGNING YOUR JOB TO MATCH YOUR ABILITIES

Let us now consider your job. Let's assume that you are highly intelligent. You may perform less well on routine and intellectually undemanding jobs than on intellectually demanding ones. How can you manage to get more of the intellectually demanding jobs?

a. First of all, take a look around and see which of your various subtasks require relatively more intellectual effort. For example, the manager of a shipping department does a lot of routine, nonintellectual work. But there are also some aspects of the job that do require intellectual effort. Would new types of addressing labels expedite the job? Is there a way of developing a computer program to find the shortest routes for delivery trucks? Can the shipping dock or preparation room be better organized?

b. Tell your boss what kind of a job you want. You may prefer to work on problem A rather than problem B, and never have told your boss. You can praise your boss for giving you intellectually demanding problems by telling him how exciting this makes the work and how much you appreciate his or her confidence when you are assigned these tasks.

IF YOU ARE NOT AN INTELLECTUAL GIANT . . .

What do you do if you feel that you have less native ability than others in your peer group? You obviously have some other talents, otherwise you would not be in your present job. Exactly what are these talents?

Are you particularly adept in handling people, in soothing ruffled feathers, in resolving conflicts among subordinates or between departments? These are extremely valuable skills. How can you best exploit them?

Obviously, you need to find a job that permits you to play your strong suits. The principles and procedures are exactly the same as those described above. You must learn to work on jobs you perform best, and to develop leadership situations that permit you to capitalize on what you have.

CAPITALIZING ON YOUR INTERPERSONAL SKILLS

Let us consider another important factor in making use of your abilities, namely, the valuable skill of dealing with difficult interpersonal situations. Again, remember that everyone likes to think he or she is especially talented in understanding and influencing people. Unfortunately, being interpersonally gifted is not everyone's strong point, and if it isn't yours, recognize it and try not to become involved in jobs in which these particular abilities are critical. Why court failure?

Let's again understand that you are not likely to be a manager if you were an interpersonal disaster. At a minimum, you will be moderately good in this area, and you may even be extremely good. Here are some landmarks to help you judge your own skill in this line:

Y   N   1.   Are you often called on to mediate conflicts between departments, or fights between some of your colleagues?

Y   N   2.   Do people come to you with their personal problems, even though they may not be related to their work? (e.g., about marital difficulties, alcohol or drug-related problems, extramarital affairs, or behavior that would get them into legal difficulties?)

Y   N   3.   Do you feel that you have many real friends you could go to in case of need? Do you, for instance, get a lot of invitations to social events and requests to serve on committees, indicating that people like and trust you?

Y   N   4.   Does your group have less absenteeism, less turnover, fewer grievances, and less conflict than is the case in other comparable units of your organization?

Y   N   5.   Do you usually get selected to speak for others, or represent them as an officer in social and professional organizations?

If you have answered most of these questions in the affirmative, you may assume that you have more ability in the interpersonal area than do others in your organization at your level.

How can you capitalize on this talent? First, note that people with high interpersonal skills do not necessarily perform better than those with less skill. As with intellectual abilities, the question is when, where, and how to use them.

Interpersonal skills are needed by leaders in jobs involving people who are troubled or under great interpersonal stress. Typically, in fact, the more intellectually able leaders do not perform too well in jobs of this type. They are too impatient and are often unable to see why people cannot act rationally in emotionally charged situations.

WHAT KINDS OF JOBS ARE APPROPRIATE FOR YOU?

Jobs which involve a lot of personal stress:

1. Jobs in which there is a great deal of interaction with people who are under stress—hospitals, restaurant staffs, air line attendants, bus drivers, police departments, etc.
2. Jobs in which conflict is built in. Program coordinators who have little or no power over those whose work they must coordinate, program managers in matrix organizations, labor relations managers, safety managers, etc.
3. Jobs in which interpersonal politics present obstacles to getting the work done efficiently, or jobs in which informal contacts enable managers to achieve their goals. A good example of this type is the army supply sergeant who is expected to "scrounge" and wheel and deal for spare parts, for replacing missing items, etc.

Again, you must get yourself into a position where these abilities are useful and valued by the organization. The procedures for doing so are identical to those we mentioned in the section on using your intellectual abilities:

1. Identify the jobs, or the aspects of your own job which demand interpersonal skills.
2. Reward your boss for giving you jobs capitalizing on your ability to manage difficult interpersonal relations.
3. Stay away from jobs you are not equipped to do well, or hand them over to others. It may be better "to have loved and lost than never to have loved at all." But it's a lot better to have loved and won!

Finally, as boss of other leaders you must consider these issues with respect to your own subordinates. Carefully analyze subordinate's jobs in order to match the person with the right skills to the right job. It is of critical importance that you recognize the impact of your own actions on the effectiveness of your group members. Not all of your people can be managed in the same way. Some may work much more effectively if you push them hard and create a stressful environment. Others may need a stress-free environment and a great deal of support from you. Since stress tends to interfere with the effective use of intelligence, create a relaxed, supportive environment for subordinates who must deal with intellectually demanding tasks. For some individuals who have a routine, nonintellectual job, some stress may be beneficial. It is important to monitor your subordinates and discuss their needs with them so that you can create the right kind of environment.

Now, try probe 28 on the next page to test your understanding of these issues.

PROBE 29

You are an account executive in an advertising agency. You have just learned that one of your largest and most profitable accounts is very dissatisfied and is considering changing agencies. They regard your company's most recent ad campaigns as dull and uncreative. You have about one month to come up with a presentation for a new campaign. Since this is not really your strong point you need to pick an account executive and a team to work on the project. After much thought you are sure that Ann Larsen is the right person for the job. She is a brilliant young woman with a very creative mind. She has, in the past, come up with some terrific ad campaigns, but she has also bombed once or twice, coming up with ideas that didn't hang together or weren't fully developed. You also know that she is a relationship-motivated leader.

You need to develop a plan on how to get this project organized and how to deal with Ann. Here are a couple of the things you have to consider:

1. What should be the composition of the creative team? You are pretty sure about most of the people, but your most creative artist, Sid, tends to be hard to get along with and sometimes can't handle too much pressure. Your next best person, Bill, is a little less creative, but much more solid. Should you put Sid or Bill on the team, or should you let Ann choose the one she wants?
2. How should you approach Ann about the project? Would it be best to tell her how critical her performance is and that failure would be disastrous? Should you intimate that her future may well be on the line? Should you encourage her to do her best but try to buffer her from the heaviest weight of the stress?

Think about your answers to these questions and then go to the next page for feedback.

FEEDBACK

1. *The decision on the composition of the team has several implications.*

    The first of these relates to overall situational control. Given the creative and demanding nature of the task, the situation is likely to be of moderate control if everything else (i.e., the leader-member relations and power) are high. Since Ann is a relationship-motivated leader, a moderate control situation would be best for her, so you want to make leader-member relations as good as possible.

    A second issue relates to stress. Since the project is an intellectually demanding and creative assignment, you want to keep stress down so that Ann can make use of her talents.

    Both of these considerations suggest that Bill would be a better choice than the volatile and unpredictable Sid. However, the best course of action would probably be to involve Ann in this decision and in the decisions about the other members of the team. Letting her have a hand in picking her subordinates is likely to result in very good leader-member relations. It also will give Ann the feeling that you are supportive of her and will project the same message to her subordinates.

2. *To stress or not to stress, that is the question.*

    The challenging and exciting nature of this project will probably provide sufficient interest to make Ann feel highly motivated. Adding additional stress through threats is most likely to interfere with Ann's ability to utilize her creative and intellectual talents. She might just get so distracted that she bombs on this one. As her boss you ought to give her the ball and then give her your protection from too much flak.

    If you had the correct answer for this probe, you are doing very well indeed. You managed to draw on all of the information we have presented. If you were unsure about your answers, you might reread this chapter and go over the probe again.

13

A FINAL NOTE

You have now completed the training program to make you a more effective leader. If you have successfully worked through all the exercises and probes, you should have a fairly good understanding of the principles that will enable you to manage your groups more productively.

Let's review a few points essential for improving your leadership performance.

First, this manual has been concerned with effective leadership. Management and leadership involve many other functions, although the direction and supervision of others is the single most important task. Leaders must also counsel their subordinates; they must provide a climate in which their subordinates can grow in professional skills, and they must try to develop a satisfied group that is motivated to work toward a common goal.

Although we have not specifically focused on improving human relations skills, available studies do indicate that Leader Match training also makes for better interpersonal performance. This was shown in the published study comparing trained and untrained Navy officers and petty officers (Leister, Borden, and Fiedler 1977), and a study of department store executive trainees who were evaluated about one year after Leader Match training.

You may or may not feel the need of further training in these areas. Having a satisfied work group is not necessarily related to good performance, but it is a goal to which we should aspire for its own sake, as well as for the sake of those who work with us.

Second, this program introduces you to a set of principles. It is not designed to be a rule book you can turn to for specific answers to every problem. This manual can make you aware of factors determining success or failure in a leadership situation. It provides you with ground rules for changing your leadership situation so that your chances for success are improved.

There is, of course, no substitute for sound judgment. An attempt to apply the principles of this program uncritically is almost certain to bring frustration and disappointment. Every leadership problem is different, and will require different strategies for successful handling. Remember too that each of your subordinates has special, individual needs that must be considered to make him or her a successful, productive employee. We cannot emphasize enough that you will need to evaluate carefully how the principles of this leadership training program need to be applied to your particular situation. The evidence from our many validation studies shows that changing the leadership situation is not difficult, although it does require some thought and close monitoring in the beginning.

You will need to practice what you have learned and observe how well the various principles and guidelines apply to your particular situation, given your particular leadership style. You will have to try out a variety of methods for managing your own leadership environment before you finally find the one that works best for you.

Third, leadership is an extremely complex relationship, and many factors determine how well a particular group operates at any one time. You, as a leader, cannot expect to control all of the many things affecting the performance of your group. You cannot singlehandedly change the state of the economy, your organization's market position, or the favor or disfavor with which the organization views your department or office. Nor can you pick your superiors and, in many cases, you cannot choose your subordinates.

However, an organization which uses a sound performance evaluation program allows you to become aware of the situations and the conditions under which you perform best. Seek out these evaluations, or develop good performance criteria for your own organizational unit, so that you can monitor and continually improve your leadership skills as well as your ability to seek and develop situations in which you and your subordinates are most likely to succeed.

You can expect your group's performance to increase considerably when the situation matches your personality. With your newly learned skills you can also expect that you can make this happen more and more frequently. And if you can improve the number of times your group performs better, you will, indeed, be way ahead of the game.

GOOD LUCK

FINAL TEST

The following questions are designed to test your overall understanding of the material presented in this book. Select the statement that best completes or answers each item. Feedback is given following the test.

_____ 1. Relationship-motivated leaders perform best in which of the following:
  a. Low control situations
  b. High control situations
  c. Moderate control situations
  d. All of the above

_____ 2. The concept of a leadership style is best summarized by:
  a. A variable, changing, almost random set of attitudes and behaviors.
  b. A set of personality traits which are associated with effective leadership.
  c. A motivational pattern or set of needs which the leader seeks to satisfy in the group-task situation.
  d. A basic behavioral pattern, such as giving orders or asking for suggestions, which the leader shows in _every_ situation.

_____ 3. A structured task is one in which:
  a. It is difficult to determine whether the job was done right.
  b. The goal or outcome is clearly stated or known.
  c. There are many ways to accomplish the task.
  d. There are many possible solutions.

_____ 4. Three variables are used to specify the situational control of a leadership position. These variables differ in importance. Which choice gives these three variables in their correct order of importance?

a. 1. leader-member relations
   2. task structure
   3. position power

b. 1. position power
   2. task structure
   3. leader-member relations

c. 1. task structure
   2. leader-member relations
   3. position power

d. 1. position power
   2. leader-member relations
   3. task structure

_____ 5. Much discussion in this program focused on methods of changing situational control. Why weren't methods of changing LPC scores discussed?

a. No one knows what LPC is.
b. Only high LPC persons can change their LPC score.
c. Only low LPC persons can change their LPC score.
d. The LPC score is a measure of stable traits that are difficult to change.

_____ 6. A manager displays the following set of behaviors: Under some stress or uncertainty in his job, he tends to seek out the support and advice of his followers. He avoids conflict and tries to create a warm interpersonal environment. He is not often punitive. He is excited by diverse and challenging problems and performs very well in such situations but becomes aloof, apathetic, and somewhat self-centered when problems and complexity are not present. This manager is likely to be a:

a. High LPC leader (relationship-motivated)
b. Low LPC leader (task-motivated)
c. He does not fit clearly into either of the above categories.

_____ 7. If you were asked to summarize briefly the most important aspect of a leaderhip situation for leaders, which of the concepts below would be most useful in classifying situations?

a. The degree to which the situation allows leaders to predict with certainty the effects of their behavior.
b. The degree to which leaders feel attracted to their subordinates and coworkers.
c. The degree to which the situation gives the leader formal power over his subordinates.
d. The potential amount of tangible rewards available to the leader and his group.

_____ 8. Leaders and managers often vary in the amount of job-related training and experience which they have. This is thought to be an important aspect of leadership. What is the impact of training and experience?

   a. Generally, training and experience make a leader more task-oriented, especially more structuring and directive.
   b. Experience and to a lesser extent, training, tend to improve markedly the performance of most leaders.
   c. Training and experience generally make the task more structured, thereby improving situational control.
   d. Training and experience usually make a leader more sensitive to the needs of his or her followers.

_____ 9. If you had a job in which the leader's situation tended to be very good in terms of support from followers, clarity of job demands, and the leader's formal and informal influence, which of the following leader types would be likely to perform best?

   a. Task-motivated
   b. Relationship-motivated
   c. Either of the above

_____ 10. Consider the situation described in the previous question (#9). Now assume that there were major changes in personnel which reduced the group's support of the leader and created group conflict and dissension. What type of leader would be likely to perform best?

   a. Task-motivated
   b. Relationship-motivated
   c. Either of the above

_____ 11. If you wish to increase situational control for a leader, which of the following courses of action would be *most* effective?

   a. Give the leader a more complex task with fewer guidelines.
   b. Allow the leader to decide who gets salary bonuses among his subordinates.
   c. Give the leader a title and greater authority.
   d. Allow the leader to choose his own subordinates from available personnel.

_____ 12. You have a leadership situation with the following characteristics: Leader-member relations are quite good and position power is moderate to high. The task has a reasonably high degree of structure but is quite complicated and requires the leader to learn quite a bit about it. The situational control of this position is likely to be:

a. Moderate for an inexperienced leader; high for an experienced leader
b. Low for an inexperienced leader; high for an experienced leader
c. Low for an inexperienced leader; moderate for an experienced leader
d. High for an inexperienced leader; moderate for an experienced leader

_____ 13. Which of the following organizational procedures is likely to decrease situational control for the organization's leaders?

a. Channeling all relevant organizational information through group leaders
b. Allowing supervisors and managers to pick their own staffs
c. A general policy of rotation
d. A broad program of supervisory and managerial training

_____ 14. The degree of control that a situation presents for the leader can be changed by modifying various aspects of the situation. Which of the following aspects, if changed, will have the most drastic effect on situational control?

a. Position power
b. Task structure
c. Leader-member relations

ANSWERS TO FINAL TEST

__c__ 1. *Relationship-motivated leaders perform best in:* Moderate control situations. Task-motivated leaders perform best in high control and low control situations. (See Chapter 8 for review.)

__c__ 2. *The concept of a leadership style is best summarized by:* A motivational pattern or set of needs which the leader seeks to satisfy in the group-task situation. Leadership style is a measure of the individual's motivational pattern and a measure of what goals in the work situation are important to them. If leadership style were a changing, random set of behaviors, this program would not be possible. (See Chapter 2 for review.)

__b__ 3. *A structured task is one in which:* The goal or outcome is clearly stated or known. This is the only choice which reflects a structured task. The other answers describe unstructured tasks. (see Chapter 5 for review.)

__a__ 4. *Three variables are used to specify the situational control of a leadership position. These variables differ in importance. These variables in their correct order of importance are:* 1. Leader-member relations; 2. task structure; and, 3. position power. Leader-member relations are twice as important as task structure, which is twice as important as position power. These weightings are reflected in the various scales which measure situational control; leader-member relations is worth forty points, task structure is worth twenty points, and position power is worth ten points. (See Chapter 7 for review.)

__d__ 5. *Much discussion in this program focused on methods of changing situational control. Methods of changing LPC scores were not discussed because:* The LPC score is a measure of stable traits that are difficult to change. LPC is a reflection of your personality and your basic leadership style. It is nearly impossible to change your personality. However, it is fairly simple to change various aspects of your leadership situation. (See Chapters 2 and 9 for review.)

__a__ 6. *A manager displays the following set of behaviors: Under some stress or uncertainty in his job, he tends to seek out the support and advice of his followers. He avoids conflict and tries to create a warm interpersonal environment. He is not often punitive. He is excited by diverse and challenging problems and performs very well in such situations, but becomes aloof, apathetic, and somewhat self-centered when problems and complexity are not present. This man-*

ager is likely to be a: High LPC leader (relationship-motivated). This is an accurate description of the high LPC (relationship-motivated) leader. If you missed this one, review the descriptions of the two kinds of leadership styles in Chapter 2.

___a___ 7. *If you were asked to summarize briefly the most important aspect of a leadership situation for leaders, the concept that would be most useful in classifying situations is:* The degree to which the situation allows leaders to predict with certainty the effects of their behavior. If leaders have high situational control, they can predict with certainty the outcome of their own and their group's behavior. This is the most important aspect of a situation for leaders. However, this should not be confused with choice (b) which is similar to leader-member relations—the most important dimension in measuring situational control. (See Chapter 3 for review.)

___c___ 8. *Leaders and managers often vary in the amount of job-related training and experience which they have. This is thought to be an important aspect of leadership. The impact of training and experience is:* Training and experience generally make the task more structured, thereby improving situational control. Experience and training will tend to improve the performance of some types of leaders. However, the best answer is that experience and training have the effect of making the task more structured for leaders, thereby increasing their control of the situation, which may or may not improve their performance. (See Chapter 5 for review.)

___a___ 9. *If you had a job in which the leader's situation tended to be very good in terms of support from followers, clarity of job demands, and the leader's formal and informal influence, the leader type that would perform best would be:* Task motivated. The situation described here is one of high control which is best suited for the task-motivated leader. (See Chapter 8 for review.)

___b___ 10. *Consider the situation described in the previous question (#9). Now assume that there were major changes in personnel which reduced the group's support of the leader and created group conflict and dissension. The type of leader who would be likely to perform best is:* Relationship-motivated. Because the leader-member relations are now poor, but with high task structure and position power, the situational control is moderate. The relationship-motivated leader performs best in this type of situation. (See Chapter 8 for review.)

___d___ 11. *If you wish to increase situational control for a leader, the course of action most effective would be:* Allow the leader to choose subordinates from available personnel. Because leader-member relations are the most important dimension in determining situational control, allowing the leader to choose subordinates from available personnel will increase his or her leader-member relations, thereby increasing his situational control. Choices (b) and (c) would also improve situational control, but not as much as a change in leader-member relations. (See Chapter 9 for review.)

__a__ 12. *You have a leadership situation with the following characteristics: Leader-member relations are quite good and position power is moderate to high. The task has a reasonably high degree of structure, but it is quite complicated and requires the leader to learn quite a bit about it. The situational control of this position is likely to be:* Moderate for an inexperienced leader; high for an experienced leader. The situation described here is one of high control for an experienced leader, but only moderate in control for the new leader. After the new leader has been on the job for quite some time, the situation will become high in control. (See Chapters 9 and 10 for review.)

__c__ 13. *The organizational procedure most likely to decrease situational control for the organization's leaders is:* A general policy of rotation. A system of general rotation is an effective way to decrease situational control within an organization. Choices (a), (b), and (d) have the effect of increasing situational control. (See Chapters 9 and 10 for review.)

__c__ 14. *The degree of control that a situation presents for the leader can be changed by modifying various aspects of the situation. The most drastic effect on situational control will result from a change in:* Leader-member relations. A change in leader-member relations will have the most effect on situational control. This is because leader-member relations are the most important dimension of situational control and worth more weight in measuring situations. (See Chapters 3, 4, and 9 for review.)

LEADER MATCH REVIEW

This is a short review of the terms and concepts presented in this book so that you can quickly refresh your memory without having to reread the entire manual. If you are fuzzy on any of the points, refer to the appropriate chapter for an intensive discussion.

First, there are two different kinds of leadership styles, which are measured by the Least Preferred Coworker (LPC) scale.

1. Relationship-motivated (high LPC, score of 73 or above) leaders tend to be most concerned with maintaining good interpersonal relations, sometimes even to the point of letting the task suffer. In relaxed, well-controlled situations, this type of person tends to reverse his or her behavior and become more task conscious.
2. Task-motivated (low LPC, score of 64 or below) leaders place primary emphasis on task performance. These leaders are the no-nonsense people who tend to work best from guidelines and specific directions. If these are lacking, their first priority is to organize and create these guidelines and then assign the various duties to their subordinates. However, under relaxed, well-controlled situations, task-motivated leaders take the time to be pleasant and pay more attention to the morale of their employees.

Leaders whose score falls between 65 and 72 will have to determine for themselves which category they most nearly resemble.

Second, there are three kinds of leadership situations:

1. High control situations allow the leader a great deal of control and influence and a predictable environment in which to direct the work of others.
2. Moderate control situations present the leader with mixed problems—either good relations with subordinates but an unstructured task and low position power, or the reverse—poor relations with group members but a structured task and high position power.
3. Low control situations offer the leader relatively low control and influence; that is, where the group does not support the leader, and neither the task nor position power give him or her much influence. Stress or high group conflict may also contribute to low control.

Third, there are three dimensions that determine the situational control of a job. These are:

1. *Leader-member relations* measure how well the group and the leader get along.
2. *Task structure* measures how clearly the procedures, goals, and evaluation of the job are defined.
3. *Position power* measures how much authority to hire and fire and discipline the leader has.

In matching leadership styles to appropriate situations we find that:

1. Relationship-motivated leaders perform best in moderate control situations.
2. Task-motivated leaders perform best in high and low control situations.
3. Socioindependent leaders tend to perform best in situations in which their control is high.

Finally, you can change or modify your leadership situation if you find that your leadership style or your abilities do not match the particular requirements of the situation in which you are working. You can engineer your job by adjusting the three dimensions of situational control and making it higher or lower, thereby matching your leadership style, and you can affect the way you interact with your boss. Transfer and rotation, selection and placement, are management tools to improve the performance of your subordinate leaders, thereby increasing organizational effectiveness.

SUGGESTED READINGS

Bass, B. M. *Stogdill's Handbook of Leadership—A survey of theory and research*, 1981, 30:489–507.

Bons, P. M., and Fiedler, F. E. The effects of changes in command environment on the behavior of relationship and task-motivated leaders. *Administrative Science Quarterly*, 1976, 21:453–473.

Chemers, M. M., and Skrzypek, G. J. An experimental test of the Contingency Model of Leadership Effectiveness. *Journal of Personality and Social Psychology*, 1972, 24:172–177.

Chemers, M. M., Rice, R. W., Sundstrom, E., and Butler, W. M. Leader esteem for the least preferred coworker score, training, and effectiveness: An experimental examination. *Journal of Personality and Social Psychology*, 1975, 31:401–409.

Csoka, L. S., and Bons, P. M. Manipulating the situation to fit the leader's style – two validation studies of LEADER MATCH. *Journal of Applied Psychology*, 1978, 63:295–300.

Fiedler, F. E. Engineer the job to fit the manager. *Harvard Business Review*, 1965, 43:116–112.

Fiedler, F. E. *A theory of leadership effectiveness*. New York: McGraw-Hill, 1967.

Fiedler, F. E. Style or circumstance: The leadership enigma. *Psychology Today*, 1969.

Fiedler, F. E. Leadership experience and leader performance—Another hypothesis shot to hell. *Organizational Behavior and Human Performance*, 1970, 5:1–14.

Fiedler, F. E. Validation and extension of the Contingency Model of leadership effectiveness: A review of empirical findings. *Psychological Bulletin*, 1971, 76:128–148.

Fiedler, F. E. *Leadership*. New York: General Learning Press, 1971.

Fiedler, F. E. How do you make leaders more effective? New answers to an old puzzle. *Organizational Dynamics*, 1972, 1:3–18.

Fiedler, F. E. The effects of leadership training and experience: A Contingency Model interpretation. *Administrative Science Quarterly*, 1972, 17:453–470.

Fiedler, F. E. Stimulus/Response: The trouble with leadership training is that it doesn't train leaders. *Psychology Today*, 1973, 6:23–92.

Fiedler, F. E. The Contingency Model—New directions for leadership utilization. *Contemporary Business*, 1974, 65–79.

Fiedler, F. E. and Chemers, M. M. *Leadership and effective management*. New York: Scott Foresman and Company, 1974.

Fiedler, F. E. The Leadership Game: Matching the man to the situation. *Organizational Dynamics*, 1976, Winter: 6–16.

Fiedler, F. E., Bell, C. H., Jr., Chemers, M. M., Patrick, D. Increasing mine productivity and safety through management training and organization development: a comparative study. *Basic and Applied Social Psychology*, 1984.

Fiedler, F. E., and Mahar, L. The effectiveness of contingency model training: A review of the validation of Leader Match. *Personnel Psychology*, 1979b, 32:45–62.

Fiedler, F. E., and Mahar, L. A field experiment validating contingency model leadership training. *Journal of Applied Psychology*, 1979a, 64(3):247–254.

Frost, D. E. Role perceptions and behavior of the immediate superior: Moderating effects on the prediction of leadership effectiveness. *Organizational Behavior and Human Performance*, 1983, 31(1):123–142.

Godfrey, E., Fiedler, F. E., and Hall, D. M. *Boards, Management and Company Success*. Danville, Illinois: Interstate Press, 1959.

Kennedy, J. K., Jr. Middle LPC leaders and the contingency model of leadership effectiveness. *Organizational Behavior and Human Performance*, 1982, 30(1):1–14.

Leister, A. P., Borden, D. F., and Fiedler, F. E. Validation of contingency model leadership training: Leader Match. *Academy of Management Journal*, 1977, 20:464–507.

McNamara, V. D. Leadership, staff and school effectiveness. Unpublished doctoral dissertation, University of Alberta, Alberta, Canada, 1968.

Strube, M. J., and Garcia, J. E. A meta-analytic investigation of Fiedler's contingency model of leadership effectiveness. *Psychological Bulletin*, 1981, 93(3):600–603.

Wexley, K. N., and Latham, G. P. *Developing and training human resources in organizations*. Glenview, Illinois: Scott, Foresman and Company, 1981.

LEADER MATCH SCALES

This Appendix includes a copy of each of the scales needed to apply the concepts of Leader Match. These scales, on perforated pages which may be easily torn out, should serve as master copies to be reproduced as needed.

LEADER-MEMBER RELATIONS SCALE

Circle the number which best represents your response to each item.

	strongly agree	agree	neither agree nor disagree	disagree	strongly disagree
1. The people I supervise have trouble getting along with each other.	1	2	3	4	5
2. My subordinates are reliable and trustworthy.	5	4	3	2	1
3. There seems to be a friendly atmosphere among the people I supervise.	5	4	3	2	1
4. My subordinates always cooperate with me in getting the job done.	5	4	3	2	1
5. There is friction between my subordinates and myself.	1	2	3	4	5
6. My subordinates give me a good deal of help and support in getting the job done.	5	4	3	2	1
7. The people I supervise work well together in getting the job done.	5	4	3	2	1
8. I have good relations with the people I supervise.	5	4	3	2	1

Total Score

TASK STRUCTURE RATING SCALE—PART 1

Circle the number in the appropriate column.	Usually True	Sometimes True	Seldom True
Is the Goal Clearly Stated or Known?			
1. Is there a blueprint, picture, model or detailed description available of the finished product or service?	2	1	0
2. Is there a person available to advise and give a description of the finished product or service, or how the job should be done?	2	1	0
Is There Only One Way to Accomplish the Task?			
3. Is there a step-by-step procedure, or a standard operating procedure which indicates in detail the process which is to be followed?	2	1	0
4. Is there a specific way to subdivide the task into separate parts or steps?	2	1	0
5. Are there some ways which are clearly recognized as better than others for performing this task?	2	1	0
Is There Only One Correct Answer or Solution?			
6. Is it obvious when the task is finished and the correct solution has been found?	2	1	0
7. Is there a book, manual, or job description which indicates the best solution or the best outcome for the task?	2	1	0
Is It Easy to Check Whether the Job Was Done Right?			
8. Is there a generally agreed upon understanding about the standards the particular product or service has to meet to be considered acceptable?	2	1	0
9. Is the evaluation of this task generally made on some quantitative basis?	2	1	0
10. Can the leader and the group find out how well the task has been accomplished in enough time to improve future performance?	2	1	0

SUBTOTAL _____

TASK STRUCTURE RATING SCALE—PART 2

Training and Experience Adjustment

NOTE: Do not adjust jobs with task structure scores of 6 or below.

a. Compared to others in this or similar positions, how much *training* has the leader had?

3	2	1	0
No training at all	Very little training	A moderate amount of training	A great deal of training

b. Compared to others in this or similar positions, how much *experience* has the leader had?

6	4	2	0
No experience at all	Very little experience	A moderate amount of experience	A great deal of experience

Add lines (a) and (b) of the training and experience adjustment, then *subtract* this from the subtotal given in Part 1.

Subtotal from Part 1.

Subtract training and experience adjustment

Total Task Structure Score

POSITION POWER RATING SCALE

Circle the number which best represents your answer.

1. Can the leader directly or by recommendation administer rewards and punishments to subordinates?

2	1	0
Can act directly or can recommend with high effectiveness	Can recommend but with mixed results	No

2. Can the leader directly or by recommendation affect the promotion, demotion, hiring or firing of subordinates?

2	1	0
Can act directly or can recommend with high effectiveness	Can recommend but with mixed results	No

3. Does the leader have the knowledge necessary to assign tasks to subordinates and instruct them in task completion?

2	1	0
Yes	Sometimes or in some aspects	No

4. Is it the leader's job to evaluate the performance of subordinates?

2	1	0
Yes	Sometimes or in some aspects	No

5. Has the leader been given some official title of authority by the organization (e.g., foreman, department head, platoon leader)?

2	0
Yes	No

Total ☐

SITUATIONAL CONTROL SCALE

Enter the total scores for the Leader-Member Relations dimension, the Task Structure scale, and the Position Power scale in the spaces below. Add the three scores together and compare your total with the ranges given in the table below to determine your overall situational control.

1. *Leader-Member Relations Total*

2. *Task Structure Total*

3. *Position Power Total*

Grand Total

Total Score	51 – 70	31 – 50	10 – 30
Amount of Situational Control	High Control	Moderate Control	Low Control

INDEX